BPMN 2.0 –
Introduction to the Standard
for Business Process Modeling

2nd Edition

Thomas Allweyer

BPMN 2.0

Introduction
to the Standard for
Business Process
Modeling

2nd, Updated and Extended Edition

Prof. Dr. Thomas Allweyer
thomas@allweyer.de

Title of the original version:
BPMN 2.0 Business Process Model and Notation. Einführung in den Standard für die Geschäftsprozessmodellierung.
3. Auflage. BoD, Norderstedt 2015.
English version: Thomas Allweyer and Diana Allweyer

Bibliographische Information der Deutschen Nationalbibliothek:
Die Deutsche Nationalbibliothek verzeichnet diese Publikation in der Deutschen Nationalbibliographie. Detaillierte bibliographische Daten sind im Internet über http://dnb.d-nb.de abrufbar.

Herstellung und Verlag:
BOD – Books on Demand, Norderstedt

ISBN: 978-3-8370-9331-5

Contents

1 BPMN – A Standard for Business Process Modeling

1.1 Why a Notation?

In order to manage business processes, they have to be described and documented. There are various possibilities to do so. The easiest way is the usage of textual or tabular descriptions. Flow chart diagrams are quite often created using presentation and graphics software. These diagrams mostly consist of small boxes and arrows, not following a defined method.

Unfortunately, this does not meet the requirements of exactly representing extensive processes with all relevant aspects, such as splitting rules, events, organizational units, data flow, etc. For this, appropriate notations are required. A notation for graphic business process modeling defines, for example, the symbols for the various process elements, their correct meaning, as well as their possible combinations.

Thus, a notation is a standardized language for the description of business processes. Everybody, who is familiar with this language, can understand models created by someone else. Furthermore, processes can be systematically analyzed, and their dynamic behavior can be simulated based on a standardized representation.

The subject of "Governance, Risk, and Compliance" (GRC) , which is getting increasingly important, also requires a standardized and complete documentation of adequate processes that makes sure that any legal and industry-specific demands with respect to risk management, quality management, and the compliance with safety rules, etc., are met.

Models also provide a basis for the development of information systems for executing and supporting business processes. Therefore, the models need a standardized structure, and they have to contain all information relevant for system development.

System-supported processes are more and more controlled by business process management systems (BPMS). These contain process engines which directly control the workflows using appropriate process models or formal process descriptions. For this purpose, the models have to meet very strict demands because they are not converted into a computer program by a human being, but directly processed by a machine.

In the course of time, several notations for process modeling emerged. These were quite often proprietary notations of special modeling tools or workflow management systems. By now, standards for executable process descriptions have been established, such as XPDL (XML Process Definition Language) [Workflow Management Coalition

2012], and BPEL (Business Process Execution Language) [OASIS 2007]. But XPDL and BPEL are no graphic notations, and their primary area of application is the definition of automated processes.

In the area of business-oriented process modeling, the notation of the event-driven process chain (EPC) is still frequently used. This notation was rather popular before the development of BPMN. However, EPC is not a standard, and many users have replaced EPC with BPMN. Today, most EPC modeling tools also support BPMN modeling.

Other standards, such as the activity diagrams of the Unified Modeling Language (UML), did not become accepted for business process modeling in practice. Their use basically remained restricted to the area of object-oriented software design, where UML is the accepted standard.

During the last years, BPMN (Business Process Model and Notation) has become accepted as the leading standard for business process modeling. The website *bpmnmatrix.github.io* contains a list of more than 50 tools which support BPMN modeling. An increasing number of websites, weblogs, and publications demonstrate the growing interest in this notation (e.g. [Debevoise and Taylor 2014], [Freund and Rücker 2014], [Herrera 2015], [Silver 2012]). Even a novel on process modeling with BPMN has been published [Grosskopf et al. 2009]. A selection of interesting internet sources can be found in the annex of this book.

Many organizations are providing their process management teams with BPMN training, and they are rolling out BPMN as their organization-wide modeling standard. In the e-government standards of Switzerland, for example, the use of BPMN is recommended as a common notation [Fischli et al. 2016]. Other examples of organizations which have published their BPMN modeling guideline documents are the public administrations of Queensland (Australia) [Queensland Government 2016] and British Columbia (Canada) [Lindner 2014]. In a recent survey on the use of BPM tools, BPMN was also the most widely used process modeling notation [Lübbe and Schnägelberger 2015].

1.2 Development of BPMN

Originally, BPMN was developed by the Business Process Management Initiative (BPMI), a consortium which consisted mainly of software companies. In the beginning, the purpose was to provide a graphical notation for process descriptions expressed in BPML (Business Process Modeling Language). Comparable to BPEL, BPML was used for specifying process descriptions which could be executed by a BPMS. BPML is not being developed further anymore; it has been given up in favor of BPEL.

The first version of the BPMN specification was developed by a team lead by Stephen A. White from IBM. It was published in 2004. In the meantime, BPMI has become a part of the Object Management Group (OMG). This organization is known for several software standards, such as the aforementioned UML (Unified Modeling Language).

In 2006, BPMN version 1.0 was officially accepted as an OMG standard. After some smaller changes in versions 1.1 and 1.2, version 2.0 brought more comprehensive changes and extensions. It was published in 2011. The latest version of the specification document, version 2.0.2 was released in 2013 [OMG 2013]. The actual content has not changed from version 2.0, as only minor corrections of the text have been made. In 2013, BPMN also became an official ISO standard [ISO 2013].

The most recent version of the BPMN specification can be found here:

www.omg.org/spec/BPMN

1.3 Contents of BPMN 2.0

For the majority of BPMN users, the most important aspect is the graphical representation of the models. BPMN provides three diagram types:

1. *Process or collaboration diagram:* In this type of diagram, the process flow can be modeled, including activities, splits, parallel flows, etc. It is also possible to show the collaboration between two or more processes with their exchanged messages. Process diagrams and collaboration diagrams are of the same diagram type. A diagram with only one process is often called process diagram, while a diagram with several interacting processes is a collaboration diagram.

2. *Choreography diagram:* Modeling of the data exchange between different partners, similar as in collaborations. However, each data exchange is modeled as an activity, so that on this level it is possible to visualize splits, loops, etc. in order to represent complex exchange protocols.

3. *Conversation diagram:* A conversation diagram is an overview of several partners and their interrelations.

The process or collaboration diagram is the most frequently used diagram type. Some BPMN tools and books are even restricted only to this type. Although it is undoubtedly the most important type, there are useful application areas for the other diagram types, as well. Therefore, they are also discussed in this book.

The BPMN specification explains the various notational elements not only verbally, but also defines them in a metamodel. The metamodel is documented with UML class diagrams that graphically show the features of the different BPMN constructs and their relationships. Such a metamodel is more accurate and definite than strictly verbal descriptions. The metamodel also has got additional language constructs that cannot be represented in graphic models. Such constructs are required, for example, by process engines to capture the necessary additional information for process execution.

The typical modeler does not need to work with the metamodel. Normally, he will use a modeling tool that only allows the creation of models complying with the specification, and thus with the metamodel. Therefore, it is rather the vendors of modeling tools, process engines, and similar software, who have to deal with the metamodel.

The metamodel is also the basis of an exchange format for BPMN models. Before BPMN 2.0 it was almost impossible to transfer BPMN models from one tool to another. Now, the specification defines a standardized exchange format. Many tool vendors support this standard format so that it is possible to exchange BPMN models not only between different modeling tools but also between a modeling tool and a BPMS. However, not all implementations of the exchange format are entirely consistent, so that sometimes there still may be problems and losses of some details.

For process automation, it needs to be defined how to execute each of the different BPMN elements. For this purpose, the specification defines execution semantics. The objective is to make sure that different process engines all interpret and execute a specific model in the same way. Like the exchange format, the execution semantics have not been implemented uniformly by all vendors, so there may be some differences when executing the same model on another process engine.

In spite of these occasional deviations, both the exchange format and the execution semantics are very useful, because otherwise model exchanges between different vendors' tools would be entirely impossible, and there would be much more differences in how process models are executed.

In the first version, the abbreviation BPMN stood for "Business Process Modeling Notation". In version 2.0, the name was changed to "Business Process Model and Notation". This name change emphasizes the fact that BPMN not only consists of the graphic notation, but also comprises the metamodel, the exchange format, and the execution semantics.

1.4   Business-Level Models and Executable Models

The origin of BPMN was in the field of process descriptions that can be performed by the process engine of a workflow or business process management system (BPMS). But the developers of BPMN claim that this notation allows for creating technical as well as business-level models. BPMN is supposed to be a common language of both, business experts and IT experts.

And in practice, BPMN is actually being used both for business-level modeling and for executable models. This becomes clear by looking at the tool market. BPMN is the predominant notation both for business process analysis tools and for modeling components of BPMS.

Although having a common notation, business-level models and technical models are quite different in practice. The main focus of business-level models is on the comprehension of the basic process flow. Thus, the usage of too many details is avoided. Conditions at the exits of a decision gateway are rather expressed in plain text than in exact formal terms. Exceptions and rare cases are quite often not modeled in detail but explained by notes and descriptions.

The source of some BPMN constructs is quite clearly the field of executable process definitions. BPMN contains among others special loop constructs, exception handling, and transactions. Programmers and IT-specialists are familiar with these subjects. Business process modelers, on the other hand, normally omit such items. In accordance to this, typical business-level models only comprise a subset of the whole notation.

Some BPMN experts recommend using the rather technical modeling constructs also in business-level models, to be able to show business-relevant exceptions and their handling in processes. Silver refers to the well-known 80-20 rule. He estimates that 80% of the costs, delays, and errors are caused by only 20% of the cases – the exceptions. Examples are cancelations, order changes, items out of stock, and timeouts [Silver 2012].

Those who want to apply BPMN for business process modeling should decide in advance which constructs should be used and how certain cases should be represented. It makes sense to document such decisions in the form of modeling conventions. Should the processes be modeled on a business level, and then be automated by a process engine, the way of transforming business-level models into models of executable processes has to be specified, i.e. how to complement, reorganize and detail the models.

The transition from business-oriented models to executable models is discussed in [Stiehl 2014].

1.5   About this Book

This book provides an introduction to the graphical notation of BPMN 2.0. Starting with a small example process, the basic BPMN elements for modeling simple flows are discussed. Step-by-step, the different BPMN concepts are introduced and explained using examples. The examples are generally intelligible business domain models, so that the reader does not need to have any specific IT know-how. There are only a few examples actually referring to process execution by a BPMS which are required for understanding some of BPMN's more technical features.

Since the main focus is on the application of the notation for business-oriented process modeling, the BPMN metamodel is not part of this book, nor are the execution semantics discussed. A comprehensive discussion of the execution semantics can be found in [Kosak et al. 2014].

This book presents the entire notation. Although as described above, not for every modeling purpose all BPMN elements will be required, modeling experts still should be familiar with the entire BPMN. Only then they can reasonably select what is required and useful for their own modeling activities.

It was taken care that the discussion of the various BPMN concepts conforms to the official BPMN specification, as much as possible. Sometimes it was necessary to interpret the descriptions from the specification to some degree. Therefore, the explanations in this book always represent the author's understanding. The author is always happy to receive feedback concerning mistakes and suggestions for improvement.

The book is an introduction to the BPMN standard. Thus, it does not discuss topics outside the standard, such as a specific methodology, the use of tools, etc. There are entirely different ways of using BPMN. Some suggestions can be found in [Silver 2012] and [Freund and Rücker 2014].

In the second edition, a new chapter has been added, containing a collection of useful modeling patterns. They provide best-practice solutions for typical problems arising in the practice of process modeling.

Apart from that, the overall structure and the main contents of the book have not been changed. The general introduction of BPMN in this chapter has been updated, as well as the bibliographical references. Several smaller improvements and minor modifications have been made throughout the book.

The book's website can be reached at *www.bpmn-introduction.com*. It contains up-to-date additions, information about BPMN's further development, as well as additional links to BPMN-related content.

2 BPMN by Example

2.1 A First BPMN Model

As a starting point, a simple BPMN process model is considered. The model of posting a job in figure 1 can be directly understood by most people who previously have been concerned with any kind of process modeling. The way of modeling is similar to well-known flow charts and activity diagrams.

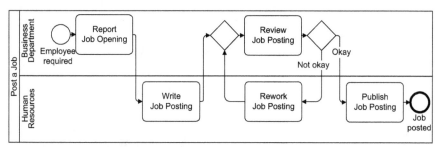

Figure 1: A simple BPMN model

A business department and the human resources department are involved in the process "Post a Job". The process starts when an employee is required. The business department reports this job opening. Then the human resources department writes a job posting. The business department reviews this job posting.

At this point, there are two possibilities: Either the job posting is okay, or it is not okay. If it is not okay, it is reworked by the human resources department. This is once more followed by the business department reviewing the job posting. Again, the result can be okay or not okay. Thus, it can happen that the job posting needs to be reviewed multiple times. If it is okay, the posting is published by the human resources department, and the end of the process is reached.

In reality, the process for creating and publishing a job posting can be much more complex and extensive. The presented example is – like all examples in this book – a simplification in order to have small and easily understandable models which can be used for explaining the different BPMN elements.

2.2 BPMN Constructs Used

Below, each element of the model in figure 1 is explained in more detail.

The entire process is contained in a pool. This is a general kind of container for a complete process. In the example above, the pool is labeled with the name of the contained process.

Every process is situated within a pool. If the pool is not important for understanding the process, it is not required to draw it in the diagram. In a process diagram which does not show a pool, the entire process is contained in an invisible, implicit pool.

Pools are especially interesting when several pools are used in order to model a collaboration, i.e. the interplay of several partners' processes. Each partner's process is then shown in a separate pool. This will be described in chapter 5.

The pool from figure 1 is partitioned into two lanes. A lane can be used for various purposes, e.g. for assigning organizational units, as in the example, or for representing different components within a technical system. In the example, the lanes show which of the process's activities are performed by the business department and which by the human resource department.

Pools and lanes are also called "swimlanes". They resemble the partitioning of swimming pools into lanes. Every participant of a competition swims only in his own lane.

The process itself begins with the start event "Employee required". Every process usually has such a start event. Its symbol is a simple circle. In most cases it makes sense to use only one start event, not several ones.

A rounded rectangle represents an activity. In an activity something gets done. This is expressed by the activities' names, such as "Report Job Opening" or "Review Job Posting".

The connecting arrows are used for modeling the sequence flow. They represent the sequence in which the different events, activities, and further elements are traversed. Often this is called control flow, but in BPMN there is a second type of flow, the message flow, which influences the control of a process as well, and is therefore some kind of control flow, too. For that reason, the term "sequence flow" is used. For distinguishing it from other kinds of flow, it is important to draw sequence flows with solid lines and filled arrowheads.

The process "Post a Job" contains a split: The activity "Review job posting" is followed by a gateway. A blank diamond shape stands for an exclusive gateway. This means that from several outgoing sequence flows, exactly one must be selected. Every time the right gateway in the job posting process is reached, a decision must be taken. Either the sequence flow to the right is followed, leading to the activity "Publish Job Posting", or the one to the left is selected, triggering the activity "Rework Job Posting". It is not possible to follow both paths simultaneously.

The logic of such a decision is also called "exclusive OR", abbreviated "XOR". The conditions on the outgoing paths determine which path is selected. If a modeling tool

Figure 2: A start event creates a token

is used and the process has to be executed or simulated by a software program, then it is usually possible to formally define exact conditions. Such formal descriptions, which may be expressed in a programming language, can be stored in special attributes of the sequence flows.

If, on the other hand, the purpose of a model is to explain a process to other people, then it is advisable to write informal, but understandable, statements directly into the diagram, next to the sequence flows. The meaning of "okay" and "not okay" after the activity called "Review Job Posting" is clear to humans – a program could not make use of it.

Gateways are also used for merging alternative paths. In the sample process, the gateway on the left of the activity "Review Job Posting" merges the two incoming sequence flows. Again, this is an exclusive gateway. It expects that either the activity "Write Job Posting" or "Rework Job Posting" is carried out before the gateway is reached – but not both at the same time. It should be taken care to use a gateway either for splitting or for joining, but not for a combination of both.

The last element in the example process is the end event. Like the start event, it has a circle as symbol – but with a thick border.

2.3 Sequence Flow Logic

The flow logic of the job posting process above is rather easy to understand. In more complex models it is sometimes not clear how the modeled structure exactly is to be interpreted. Therefore, it is helpful if the meaning of the sequence flow's elements is defined in an unambiguous way.

The logic of a process diagram's sequence flow can be explained by "tokens". Just as in a board game tokens are moved over the board according to the game's rules, one can imagine moving tokens through a process model according to BPMN's rules.

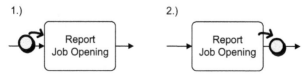

Figure 3: An activity receives a token and forwards it after completion

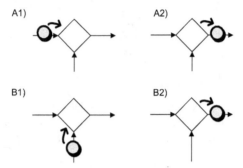

Figure 4: Routing of a token by a merging exclusive gateway

Every time the process is started, the start event creates a token (cf. figure 2). Since the job posting process is carried out more than once, many tokens can be created in the course of time. Thereby it can happen that the process for one job posting is not yet finished, when the process for posting another job starts. As it moves through the process, each token is independent from the other tokens' movements.

The token that has been created by the start event moves through the sequence flow to the first activity. This activity receives a token, performs its task (in this case it reports a job opening), and then releases it to the outgoing sequence flow (cf. figure 3).

The following activity forwards the token, too. It then arrives at the merging exclusive gateway. The task of this gateway is simple: It just takes a token that arrives via any incoming sequence flow and moves it to the outgoing sequence flow. This is shown in figure 4. In case A, a token arrives from the left, in case B from below. In both cases, the token is routed to the outgoing sequence flow to the right.

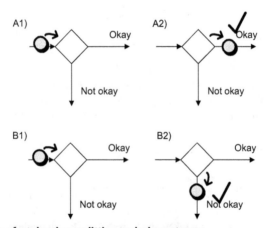

Figure 5: Routing of a token by a splitting exclusive gateway

18

Figure 6: An end event removes an arriving token

The task of the splitting exclusive gateway is more interesting. It takes one arriving token and decides according to the conditions, to which sequence flow it should be moved. In case A in figure 5, the condition "okay" is true, i.e. the preceding review activity has produced a positive result. In this case, the token is moved to the right. Otherwise, if the condition "not okay" is true, the token is moved to the downwards sequence flow (case B).

The modeler must define the conditions in such a way that always exactly one of the conditions is true. The BPMN specification does not state how to define conditions and how to check which conditions are true. Since the considered process is not executed by software, the rather simple statements used here are sufficient. Otherwise, it would be necessary to define the conditions according to the requirements and rules of the software tool.

The token may travel several times through the loop for reworking the job posting. Finally, it arrives at the end event. This simply removes any arriving token and thus finishes the entire process (figure 6).

The sequence flow of every process diagram can be simulated in this way with the help of tokens. This allows for analyzing whether the flow logic of a process has been modeled correctly.

It should be noted that a token does not represent such a thing as a data object or a document. In the case of the job posting process, it could be imagined to have a document "job posting" flowing through the process. This document could contain all required data, such as the result of the activity "Review Job Posting". At the splitting gateway, the decision could then be based on this attribute value. However, the BPMN sequence flow only represents the order of execution. The tokens therefore do not carry any information, other than a unique identifier for distinguishing the tokens from each other. For data objects, there are separate BPMN constructs which will be presented in chapter 10.

2.4 Presentation Options

Usually, pools are drawn horizontally. The preferred direction of sequence flow is then from left to right. On the other hand, it is also possible to use vertical pools and to draw the sequence flow from top to bottom, as in the example in figure 7.

19

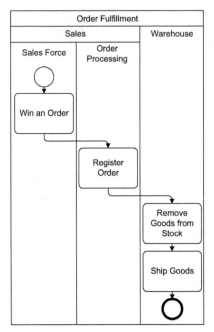

Figure 7: Vertical swimlanes and nested lanes

It makes sense to decide for only one of these possibilities – horizontal or vertical. Nevertheless, there are modeling tools which only support horizontal modeling.

Figure 7 also shows an example of nested lanes. The lane labeled "Sales" is partitioned into the two lanes "Sales Force" and "Order Processing". In principle, it is possible to partition these lanes again, and so forth, although this only makes sense up to a certain level of depth.

It is not prescribed where to put the names of pools and lanes. Typical are the variants selected for figure 1 and figure 7. Here the names are placed on the left of the pools or lanes, or at the top for the vertical style, respectively. The name of a pool is separated by a line. The names of the lanes, however, are placed directly in the lanes. A separation line is only used for a lane that is partitioned into further sub-lanes.

Lanes can also be arranged as a matrix. The procurement process in figure 8 runs through a business department and the procurement department, both of which span a branch office and the headquarters. When a demand occurs in a branch's business department, this department reports the demand. In the next step, the procurement is approved by the same department in the headquarters. The central part of the procurement department then closes a contract with a supplier, followed by the branch's purchasing department carrying out the purchase locally.

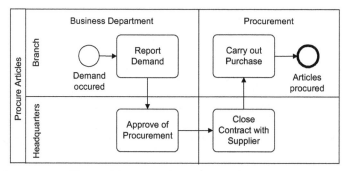

Figure 8: Lanes arranged in a matrix

Although the BPMN specification explicitly describes the possibility of such a matrix presentation, it is hardly ever applied, so far. Probably not many people are aware of this structure, nor do common BPMN modeling tools support it. Nevertheless, in many cases the matrix structure would provide a useful visualization.

Lanes can not only be used for organizational units or roles. They can be applied for categorizing a process's activities according to any kind of criteria. In figure 9, the job posting process from the beginning is partitioned not anymore according to organizational units, but according to the information systems used.

In the BPMN specification – like in this book – all elements are printed in black and white. However, it is also allowed to color the models as desired. Colors can be used for creating models that are optically more appealing. Moreover, colors can be applied in order to mark elements according to certain criteria. As an example, very important elements can be highlighted, or critical elements can be colored red.

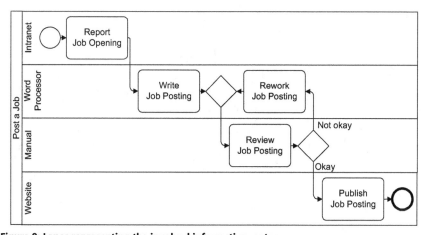

Figure 9: Lanes representing the involved information systems

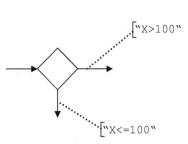

Figure 10: BPMN elements can be provided with additional information

Other graphical extensions are also possible, e.g. different kinds of activities can be marked with catchy symbols. Any changes are allowed that do not change the standard symbols' essence. Thus, it would not be permitted to use a circle as a symbol for an activity since it would not be recognizable as an activity anymore. In contrast, if the rounded rectangle would be complemented with an additional icon, every BPMN expert still would recognize that the symbol denotes an activity.

2.5 Appending Additional Information

A BPMN model's elements are not only graphical symbols. They can be appended with additional information, such as simple attributes or additional elements which are not shown in the diagram. The BPMN metamodel defines for all types of elements several possible types of additional information. To a large extent, this information is rather technical, and it is mainly needed for process execution by a process engine. For example, it is possible to add formal expressions to sequence flows in order to define conditions for selecting an outgoing sequence flow. This enables the process engine to evaluate the conditions and pick the correct exit of the gateway.

In figure 10, such conditions are shown as annotations at the outgoing sequence flows of a gateway. In BPMN, an annotation is preceded by an opening square bracket which is connected to the referred element by a dotted line. When using a modeling tool, attribute values and other additional information are usually not shown in the diagram. Instead, it may be possible to open a dialog for each element in which such information can be displayed and edited.

Although many other modeling notations comprise attributes for business related information, such attributes cannot be found in the BPMN specification. Attributes for times, cost rates, capacities, etc. are not defined. However, it is possible to define individual extensions for BPMN elements. On the other hand, individually defined extensions are not standardized. Therefore, it is hard to compare models containing such extensions. The features of modeling tools also may restrict the possibilities for defining one's own extensions.

3 Gateways: Splitting and Merging

Gateways are used for splitting and joining sequence flows. In addition to exclusive gateways already mentioned in chapter 2, further gateway types exist: the parallel gateway for modeling several parallel paths, the inclusive gateway for choosing one or more paths, and the complex gateway which is used for splits and joins according to complex rules.

3.1 Exclusive Gateway

The exclusive gateway is used for modeling alternative paths. It is applied either as a split or a merge. As shown in figure 11, there are two symbols for representing an exclusive gateway: a blank diamond shape, or a diamond shape with a large "X". It is recommended to consistently use only one of these variants. In this book, the empty diamond shape is used.

It is not forbidden to have a gateway with both multiple inputs and multiple outputs, but such a combination of a split and a merge might lead to misinterpretation. Therefore, this is not recommended. It is better to separate splits and merges (cf. figure. 12). This also applies to the other gateway types presented below, not only to the exclusive gateway.

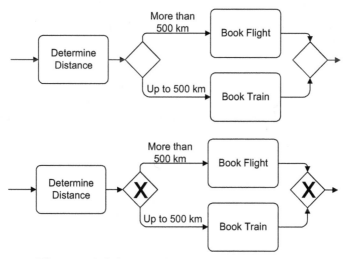

Figure 11: Two different symbols for the exclusive gateway

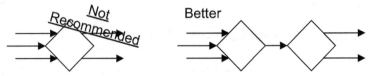

Figure 12: A single gateway should not be used simultaneously for merging and splitting

Furthermore, it should be considered that a gateway represents only logic, i.e. no activity is carried out, and no time passes while running through a gateway. This applies to any kind of gateway. If an activity is modeled that should take a decision, it is represented as an activity followed by an exclusive gateway (cf. figure 13). Another possibility to model this case is shown in chapter 4.1.

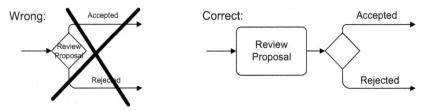

Figure 13: A gateway only represents logic, but not an action

A splitting exclusive gateway may have multiple exits between which a decision has to be taken. Either the conditions are noted in plain text at the exiting sequence flows, or they are stored in attributes in the form of logic expressions. The latter can be evaluated by process engines.

Many flowcharts use a representation as in figure 14, where the question is located in the gateway symbol, and the sequence flows only carry the answers "yes" and "no". The BPMN specification does not explicitly mention this representation. However, since the specification contains some figures with this kind of modeling, it might be at least applied as concise representation in business-level models. If the text is too long or the symbol with "X" is used, the question can also be noted next to the gateway symbol.

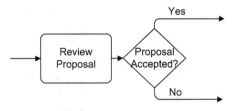

Figure 14: Question in gateway symbol

Figure 15: A gateway can have any number of exits

As already mentioned, the XOR logic of this gateway type requires exactly one condition to be true. If the condition of the bottom sequence flow was "amount < 200 €" instead of "amount < 100 €" in figure 15, this rule would be violated because both the bottom exit and the second lowest exit would have to be selected for amounts between 100 € and 200 €.

One of the exits can also be defined as default exit. The default exit is only selected if no condition from the remaining exits is true. The default is marked with a small diagonal slash. Thus, the example from figure 15 can also be modeled as in figure 16.

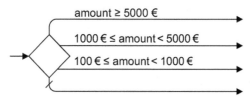

Figure 16: The bottom exit is marked as default exit

If an exclusive gateway as in figure 17 is used for merging, it must be ensured that every time only one entrance receives a token. This can be achieved by modeling the preceding split with an exclusive gateway, too.

The splitting exclusive gateway selects the exit by evaluating data. Thus, it is called "data-based exclusive gateway". There is also a so-called "event-based exclusive gateway", which will be presented in chapter 6.

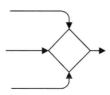

Figure 17: Merging exclusive gateway

3.2   Parallel Gateway

A parallel gateway can split a sequence flow into two or more parallel paths. This corresponds to a logical "AND". Parallel paths are also joined by a parallel gateway. A parallel gateway is represented by a diamond shape carrying a plus sign.

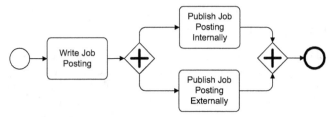

Figure 18: Usage of parallel gateways

In figure 18, a job posting is written, first. Then, the job posting is published internally as well as externally. Thus, the activities "Publish Job Posting Internally" and "Publish Job Posting Externally" both have to be carried out. Nevertheless, a special order is not prescribed, so that the job posting can be published first internally and then externally, or vice versa – or the two activities can be carried out simultaneously.

The logic of a parallel gateway can also be visualized by the flow of tokens. If a token reaches a splitting parallel gateway, it will be duplicated. Every outgoing sequence flow generates a token (cf. figure 19).

Figure 19: A splitting parallel gateway duplicates the tokens

Figure 20 represents the logic of a joining parallel gateway. When a token arrives via one of the incoming sequence flows, it is not directly passed on (left). Instead, it is waited until a token has arrived at each entrance (center). Only then the tokens of all entrances are processed. They are joined again to one token which is then emitted by the gateway's only exit (right).

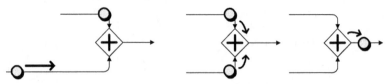

Figure 20: A joining parallel gateway waits for all arriving tokens and merges them into one token

3.3 Different Process Instances at a Parallel Join

Using the example from figure 18, it is easy to understand the concept of different process instances. Each activation of a process is represented by a new process instance. The model from figure 18 is a process definition. Here it is defined how a job posting is created in general.

If a job posting is created for a specific open position, e.g. for a purchasing agent, this single execution of the general process is a process instance.

This can be related to the idea of the token flow: Each time a start event produces a new token, a new process instance is created. Thus, at the beginning a token represents a process instance. If a token is duplicated by a parallel gateway, the resulting two or more tokens still belong to the same process instance. They are a kind of partial tokens of the original token. A joining parallel gateway fuses them together again to the original token.

At the joining parallel gateway, it is not sufficient that each entrance receives an arbitrary token. Instead, the tokens must be partial tokens that belong together. This is

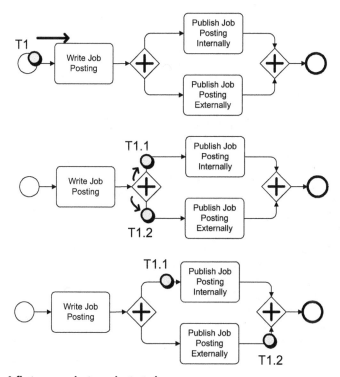

Figure 21: A first process instance is started

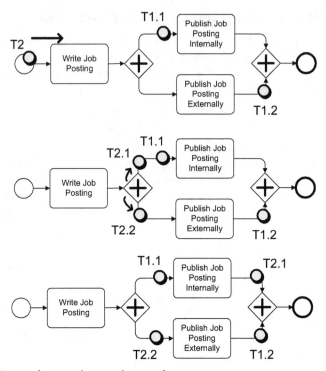

Figure 22: A second process instance is created

important if several process instances are executed simultaneously. In the example, several job postings may be created at the same time.

In figure 21, a token T1 is created (top). This token is duplicated at the parallel gateway. The resulting tokens are labeled T1.1 and T1.2 (center). Now the job posting is published externally. The internal publication is not yet done. Thus, token T1.2 resides at the joining parallel gateway. Here the process must wait until token T1.1 has arrived, as well (bottom).

In this situation, a second instance of the same process is created, because a second job posting is required. This is shown in figure 22. A second token T2 is produced. This token is also duplicated at the splitting parallel gateway; the tokens T2.1 and T2.2 are created (center). The second job posting is first published internally; the external publication takes longer. At that time, the first job posting – for whatever reasons – has still not been published internally. Therefore token 1.1 still is at the entrance of the activity "Publish Job Posting Internally". Token T2.1, in contrast, has reached the joining parallel gateway (bottom).

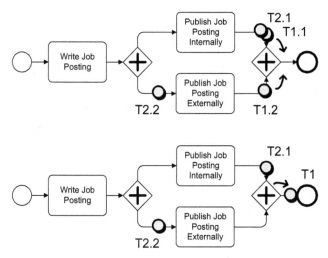

Figure 23: The process will not be continued until all tokens of a process instance have arrived

Now there are tokens at both gateway entrances. Nevertheless, these two tokens are not joined and passed on, since these partial tokens belong to different process instances. In this example, they are related to different job postings.

Figure 23 shows the next step: The first job posting has finally been published internally, i.e. token T1.1 moves to the parallel gateway. Now both partial tokens T1.1 and T1.2 of process instance T1 are in front of the parallel gateway (top). They are joined to token T1 which is then forwarded to the end event (bottom). Token T2.1 still waits for token T2.2, until these two partial tokens are also joined and moved on.

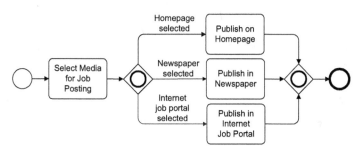

Figure 24: At a splitting inclusive gateway, one or more sequence flows are selected

3.4 Inclusive Gateway

An inclusive gateway selects or merges one or more paths. In figure 24, media need to be chosen for publishing a job posting. The company's homepage, a newspaper, and an internet job portal can be selected. Any combination with at least one of these options is possible. If no medium were selected, the posting would not be published at all. An inclusive gateway, therefore, represents the logic of an (inclusive) OR.

A merging inclusive gateway waits for all those related tokens that still can arrive according to the previous sequence flow logic. If only one sequence flow is selected in a splitting inclusive gateway, i.e. for example either the homepage or the newspaper, only one token can arrive at the merging gateway. Thus, when the token has arrived, it will be immediately passed (figure 25). In this case, the merging inclusive gateway behaves like an exclusive gateway which also passes on one single token after its arrival.

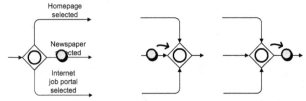

Figure 25: Inclusive gateway – one path selected

If, however, two or three sequence flows are selected at the splitting point, the behavior of an exclusive gateway would be unsuitable because it would generate a new token each time one token arrives, so that these tokens would not be merged, but two or three tokens would be passed on, one after the other.

If all of an inclusive gateway's sequence flows are selected, the merging inclusive gateway behaves like a parallel gateway, because there must be a token at each entrance before one token is passed on. In the second and third picture of figure 26, only one and two tokens have arrived at the merging point. The gateway waits for the arrival of the third and last token. Only then it will consume these three tokens, emitting a new token.

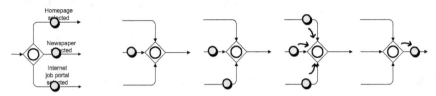

Figure 26: Inclusive gateway – all three paths selected

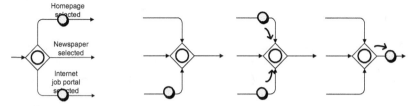

Figure 27: Inclusive gateway – two out of three paths selected

However, if only one or two sequence flows are selected at the split, a parallel gateway would lead to a blockade at the merging point because it only switches when all three tokens have arrived. This, however, will never be the case because only one or two tokens have been launched.

Figure 27 shows a case in which two sequence flows have been selected. Here, the inclusive gateway switches when both tokens have arrived. Thus, the inclusive gateway does always know how many and which sequence flows have been selected. So it knows which tokens are to be expected before it can finally launch its token.

The example in figure 28 is slightly different. Here, one of the sequence flows from the splitting inclusive gateway leads to an end event. Consequently, the token in question does not arrive at the merging gateway. This model is correct, nevertheless. A merging inclusive gateway is waiting for all tokens that belong together and might reach it. Since one token in the top branch is absorbed by the end event, and thus cannot reach the merging point, the merging inclusive gateway will not wait for it.

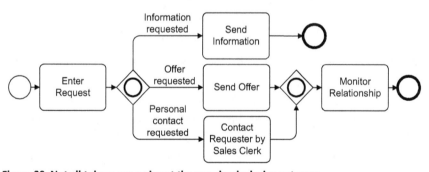

Figure 28: Not all tokens can arrive at the merging inclusive gateway

If only information is requested in the inquiry, it will be sent, and the process is finished. If an offer or personal advice or both are requested, the respective activity is carried out, and the merging inclusive gateway waits for the one or two tokens. If in parallel to the offer and/or personal advice, additional information is requested, the merge will remain unchanged. Since there is no path between information request and the merging point, the gateway is only waiting for the one or two tokens of the bottom paths.

As in the exclusive gateway, sequence flows going out from the splitting inclusive gateway are labeled with conditions. In contrast, to exclusive gateways not *exactly* one condition must apply, but *at least* one. Two or more conditions can also apply at the same time.

Therefore, an inclusive gateway can, in principle, also be used for the merging of sequence flows originating from splitting exclusive or parallel gateways. However, this is not a good modeling style. For alternative or parallel sequence flows the respective gateway should be used.

It is possible to use an inclusive gateway for merging sequence flows that were created by a combination of various gateways. Of course, the combination of exclusive and parallel gateways in figure 29 can also be used in reverse order for merging. The usage of an inclusive gateway makes the presentation slightly more compact. The preferred variant depends on the modeling style.

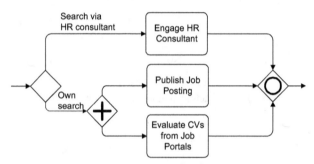

Figure 29: Inclusive gateway for merging sequence flows from a combination of gateways

Just like an exclusive gateway, an inclusive gateway can also have one of its exits marked with a small diagonal slash as the default sequence flow (cf. figure 30). It will be selected automatically if no condition of the other sequence flows is true. This ensures the actual selection of at least one sequence flow.

In contrast to the other sequence flows, the default sequence flow cannot be selected in combination with other sequence flows, because the default is only being selected if *none* of the other conditions applies. Thus, in figure 30 either any single sequence flow can be selected, or the top two sequence flows are selected. However, it is not possible to select the sequence flow at the bottom in combination with one or two of the top sequence flows. This logic is appropriate to the matter displayed. Either the job application is complete. Then the applicant will be invited. Or certificates, missing information, or both have to be requested. If something has to be requested, the applicant will not be invited at the same time.

Figure 30: Default sequence flow at an inclusive gateway

This example could also have been modeled without a default sequence flow, but with a preceding exclusive gateway, as in figure 31. This kind of presentation, however, is more complex and thus more difficult to understand. Furthermore, the modeled decisions surely do not correspond to the decision succession in practice. It is not reasonable to decide first, whether the application is complete (one had to prove that neither certificates nor important information are missing), and in case it is not complete, to decide again which of the two contents are missing. Instead, it would be reasonable to take only one decision, as descriptively shown in figure 30 using a default sequence flow.

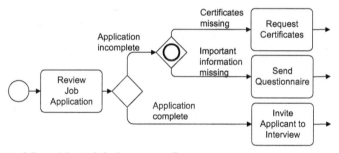

Figure 31: Modeling without default sequence flow

3.5   Complex Gateway

In figure 32, the sequence flow of an application process is split into three parallel flows by a parallel gateway. A reference for an applicant is requested in each of the three branches, two references from different employers, and one of a university professor. In fact, only two references are required. However, just to be on the safe side, three references are asked for because sometimes it takes a little bit longer for an answer to arrive. As soon as two references have been received, the process is continued. The last incoming reference will be ignored, which means the respective token will be consumed without passing another token.

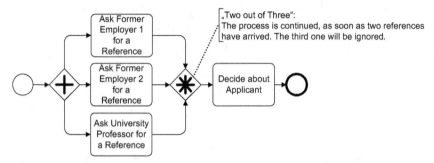

Figure 32: Merging complex gateway

There is no straightforward way to express such a complex logic using the gateway types presented above. Therefore, a complex gateway with a star symbol is used. A complex gateway may comprise any arbitrary rules for processing the arriving tokens. In figure 32, the applied rule is represented in the form of an annotation. If software tools are used for modeling, such a rule is quite often stored in an attribute of the complex gateway.

Complex gateways can not only be used for merging, but also for splitting sequence flows.

In general, complex gateways play a relatively small role among the BPMN elements. However, for very complex sequence flow rules, complex gateways can be quite helpful. A labeled complex gateway with a comprehensible label improves the model's readability and should be preferred to a complicated combination of a number of gateways.

4 Splitting and Merging without Gateways

Each of the activities in the examples above had exactly one incoming and one outgoing sequence flow. Splitting and merging of sequence flows was performed by gateways. However, it is quite often possible to lead several sequence flows directly into an activity, or to lead several sequence flows out of an activity. This enables the gateways to be replaced, leading to a concise representation.

4.1 Splitting without Gateways

Figure 33 shows two possibilities for modeling an inclusive split: On top, the already known representation with an inclusive gateway; in the presentation below, the preceding activity itself has got various exits. The sequence flows leaving the activity "Select Media for Job Posting" are so-called "conditional sequence flows". They are marked with small condition diamonds at the beginning, which means that they must be provided with conditions. The completion of an activity activates those sequence flows that have true conditions.

Since several conditions can be true at the same time, several sequence flows can be activated simultaneously. The modeler has to express the condition in such a way, that

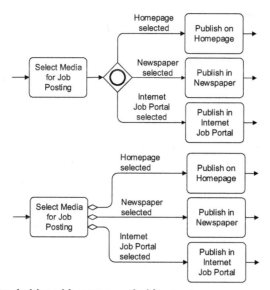

Figure 33: Inclusive decision with gateway and without gateway

at least one condition applies. Thus, the logic is exactly the same as in an inclusive gateway.

Condition diamonds are placed only at an activity's exit. If an inclusive gateway is used, the exits are automatically conditional sequence flows, thus making a further marking unnecessary.

An exclusive splitting gateway can be represented in the same way by conditional sequence flows leading out of an activity. Figure 34 shows the same exclusive split with and without a gateway. The difference to an inclusive split is that the conditions must be defined in such a way that always exactly one condition is true.

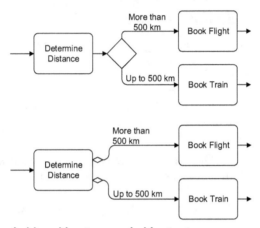

Figure 34: Exclusive decision with gateway and without gateway

In the second case, however, the modeler is not restricted to using mutually exclusive conditions – other than in the first case with the exclusive gateway. In the upper part of figure 34, a change of the second condition "Up to 500 km" into "Up to 600 km" would be a modeling mistake because both conditions would apply for distances between 500 and 600 kilometers so that the two sequence flows would not be exclusive anymore.

This would be absolutely correct in the second case of figure 34, where the exclusive split would become an inclusive one. In the end, conditional sequence flows after activities always represent the logic of inclusive gateways. Inclusive gateways may also have mutually exclusive conditions, thus creating exclusive splits. In this case, however, the split's exclusiveness in the model cannot be recognized so clearly, because the conditions have to be analyzed, first. The graphic model would lose in expressiveness; modeling faults would easily be overlooked. This also applies to the modeling with conditional sequence flows, because the exact equivalent to an exclusive gateway does not exist.

When activities are followed by conditional sequence flows, one of the sequence flows can be marked as default flow. It will be chosen automatically if no condition of the other sequence flows applies (cf. figure 35).

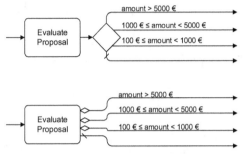

Figure 35: Default sequence flow at a gateway and an activity

If two or more normal sequence flows without condition diamonds are leaving an activity, they will all be activated as soon as the activity has been finished, thus generating a token for each exit. Therefore, it is equivalent to the usage of parallel gateways. Figure 36 shows the same parallel split with and without a gateway.

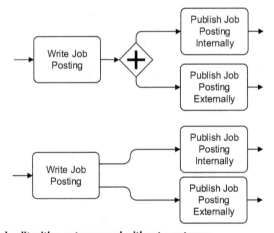

Figure 36: Parallel split with a gateway and without a gateway

Normal and conditional sequence flows can also leave an activity together. Then, each sequence flow without condition diamond generates a token – the others only if their conditions are true. In this case, however, none of the exits should be marked as default flow, because it would never be selected since there are other exits that always generate a token.

4.2 Merging without Gateways

Merging alternative paths can also be modeled without gateways. In the bottom picture of figure 37, the splitting, as well as the merging exclusive gateways, have been replaced. In this case, the alternative sequence flows directly go into the next activity. Each single token that arrives at an activity – via any entry - will directly be processed by this activity. The activity will not wait for any other tokens, and the tokens will not be merged. This behavior is appropriate for merging exclusive sequence flows where only one token can arrive.

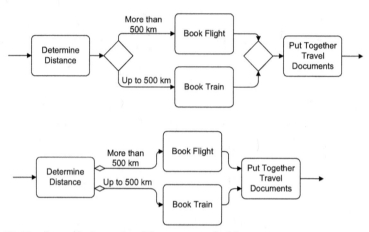

Figure 37: Merging exclusive paths with gateway and without gateway

Of course, splits and merges with and without gateways can be combined with each other. It is possible, for example, to have several conditional sequence flows leaving an activity, and to merge them later on with an exclusive gateway (cf. figure 38, top).

It must be taken care that the conditions of the conditional sequence flows are mutually exclusive, so that actually only one token can arrive at the exclusive gateway. In the same way, sequence flows originating from a splitting exclusive gateway can be merged without a gateway (cf. figure 38, bottom).

The joining of non-exclusive paths, however, cannot be modeled without a gateway. The model in figure 39 is not correct. When the activity "Write Job Posting" is finished, it emits two related tokens, one to each of the outgoing sequence flows.

The incoming sequence flows of the activity "Select Applicant", on the other hand, behave as described above: Each time a token arrives, the activity "Select Applicant" is triggered. Thus, this activity is performed twice: Once for the token from the upper sequence flow, and once for the token from the lower sequence flow.

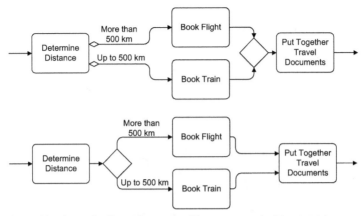

Figure 38: Combinations of splits and merges with gateway and without gateway

The resulting behavior is shown in figure 40. Here, the models at the top and the bottom represent the same thing: The activity "Select Applicant" is performed twice – when the activity "Publish Job Posting Internally" is finished, and when the parallel activity "Publish Job Posting Externally" is finished. Thus, this model does not correspond to a merging parallel or inclusive gateway. Such a gateway would wait for both related tokens and join them into a single token so that the following activity "Select Applicant" would be performed only once.

In special cases, the behavior according to figure 40 may be desired. In this case, the model at the top may be chosen as a simple representation. Here, each token flows independently to the end event. Other than in the model at the bottom, it would not be possible to rejoin the two related tokens again. Therefore, there will not be many situations for applying this model structure.

At a normal join of parallel paths, the different tokens are rejoined into one token. Regardless whether the parallel paths have been created by a parallel gateway or by multiple exits of an activity, they must be joined by a parallel or an inclusive gateway (cf. figure 41). For easier comprehension, the parallel gateway should be preferred, because it clearly indicates that each gateway entrance must receive a token.

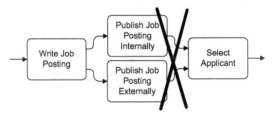

Figure 39: Non-exclusive paths cannot be merged without a gateway

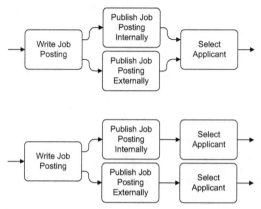

Figure 40: If several non-exclusive paths end in one activity, this activity is carried more than once

Non-exclusive paths can also be created by inclusive splits. These can be modeled not only with splitting inclusive gateways but also with an activity and several outgoing conditional sequence flows if the conditions are not mutually exclusive.

The inclusive paths in figure 42 cannot be merged without a gateway (unless multiple activations of the following activity are desired, as described above). Here again, more than one token can arrive. In this case, only a merging inclusive gateway can be used.

The behavior of multiple sequence flows going into an activity is *not* symmetrical to that of multiple sequence flows coming out of an activity. Multiple outgoing sequence flows without conditions form parallel paths; several related tokens are emitted (figure 43, left). This corresponds to a parallel gateway. However, multiple incoming sequence flows must be exclusive, i.e. only one token must arrive. This corresponds to an exclusive gateway.

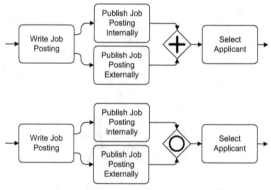

Figure 41: Correct merging of non-exclusive paths

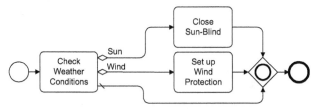

Figure 42: Merging of inclusive paths requires an inclusive gateway

This asymmetry is not intuitive; the model in figure 39 looks rather plausible for anyone who is not a BPMN expert. The different meanings of the split and the merge need to be considered in order to avoid modeling mistakes.

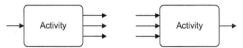

Figure 43: Multiple exits from one activity define parallel paths; multiple incoming flows are used for merging exclusive paths

4.3 Modeling with or without Gateways?

Since there are two ways of modeling splits and merges, a modeler must decide which style to use: with or without gateways?

It is not possible to model entirely without gateways. On the one hand, non-exclusive paths usually need to be merged by gateways. One the other hand, gateways are often required before or after other gateways (cf. figure 44).

If gateways are omitted as far as possible, more compact and smaller models can be created. For some cases, the modeling of splits with an activity and conditional sequence flows may also be considered as a more natural way of modeling. If a decision is made in the activity, such as in figure 45, it seems obvious to lead the different paths directly out of the activity. If the split is modeled with a gateway, it is optically separated from the deciding activity. In this case, the deciding activity pro-

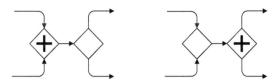

Figure 44: When a merge is followed directly by a split of another type, both gateways are required

41

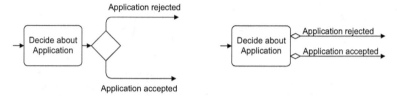

Figure 45: Different possibilities for modeling decisions

vides a result, which will be evaluated afterward for selecting one or more sequence flows.

In the case of an automated process, the process engine calls a function. It receives back a value from that function, and then it selects the correct sequence flow. Here, the separation of activity and split is suitable, because the process engine is a controlling unit which executes the process logic independently from the called functions. If no process engine is used, however, the deciding activity often is closely connected with the process control. The activity may directly trigger the following activity, or the decision maker forwards the process documents to different persons, based on the result of his decision.

If the purpose of the preceding activity is not to make a decision but to calculate a price, for example, a gateway is more suitable. The activity provides a result (e.g. a price). The following gateway can then select a sequence flow based on that price. The conditions (e.g. exceeding a certain amount) are entirely independent of the previous activity (cf. figure 46). After a decision activity, on the other hand, the conditions at the outgoing sequence flows usually correspond to the possible results of the decision (e.g. "approval" or "rejection").

The distinction between deciding activities and other activities is purely based on the modeled content, and it can be discussed whether it is useful. BPMN does not make such a distinction. It is a matter of the modeling style whether to make that distinction and model the splits in different ways or not. If required, it can be specified in modeling conventions.

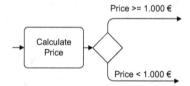

Figure 46: The activity "Calculate Price" provides a result which is then evaluated at the gateway

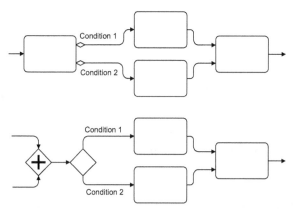

Figure 47: Decision and merge in a symmetrical way, both without gateway (top). In the second case, this is not possible since the decision is preceded by another gateway instead of another activity.

Since it is not possible to omit gateways completely, there are often asymmetrical model structures when modeling splits and merges directly at the activities. Especially non-exclusive paths must always be merged with a gateway, as it is shown in figure 41. Sometimes, exclusive splits also must be modeled with a gateway, e.g. when the split directly follows an event or another gateway (cf. figure 47).

The corresponding splits and merges are easier to detect if the same gateway types are used symmetrically. Especially in more complex cases with several combined gateways, the symmetrical use of gateways helps to understand the flow logic (cf. figures 48 and 49).

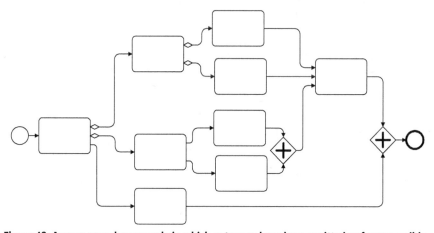

Figure 48: A more complex example in which gateways have been omitted as far as possible

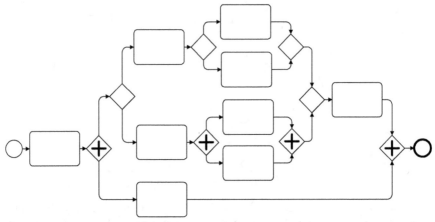

Figure 49: It is easier to understand the logic of the sequence flow if the gateways are used in a symmetrical way

Moreover, the different gateway types are more expressive. If an exclusive gateway is used, it is clear that in every case exactly one sequence flow will be selected. If the conditions at the sequence flows are not mutually exclusive, this is a clear modeling mistake. It is also a mistake if there are cases in which no condition becomes true.

If an exclusive split is modeled with conditional sequence flows after an activity, it is hard to recognize that always exactly one path is being selected. It can only be detected by analyzing the conditions at each sequence flow. If the modeler made a mistake and created conditions which are not exclusive in every case, this semantic mistake is harder to detect, because there is no violation of the BPMN syntax rules.

The model on the right side of figure 50 obviously contains a mistake: For children between 12 and 14 years, both conditions are true. This is not allowed for an exclusive gateway. In the case shown on the left, this is not forbidden, so this model is formally correct. The modeled content, of course, still does not make sense.

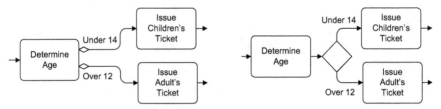

Figure 50: More expressive modeling with a gateway: In the right model, the use of over-lapping conditions is a modeling mistake

In the end, every modeler has to decide how to handle the different possibilities for modeling splits and merges. Modeling conventions should be used for achieving a uniform modeling style in a project or an enterprise.

5 Collaborations

Other than most graphical process notations, BPMN provides special means for modeling collaborations. A collaboration is a synchronized interaction of two or more processes without central control. The processes communicate by exchanging messages.

Such an interaction is also called "choreography". There is also a specific BPMN diagram type, the choreography diagram. Such a diagram also shows the interaction of several partners, but in a different way. In order to distinguish the two possible representations of interactions, the modeling style introduced in this chapter will always be referred to as "collaboration". Choreography diagrams will be presented in chapter 11.

Collaboration diagrams are especially useful for documenting the co-operation of several companies. The purchasing process of a customer and the order fulfillment process of a supplier are two independent processes. However, they are connected. In the purchasing process, an order is sent which triggers the supplier's order fulfillment process. Then this process sends an order confirmation as a reply, and so on.

Collaborations are modeled with two or more pools. Each pool contains a separate process. Between the processes, message flows are modeled. A pool does not need to represent a company, but it can also stand for a computer program or a technical system, for example. Therefore, not all collaborations represent interactions between enterprises. It is also possible to model something like a collaboration in which several independent computer programs exchange data.

5.1 Example of a Collaboration

Figure 51 shows an example of a model with a collaboration. It presents the interaction between an applicant and an enterprise in the process of a job application.

Separate pools are used for applicant and enterprise. By this, it is expressed that both participants of the collaboration are independent of each other. The applicant cannot influence the enterprise's way of processing a job application, nor can the enterprise determine what the applicant does concerning the application. And, of course, there is no central authority that would define and control the entire process that spans the two participants.

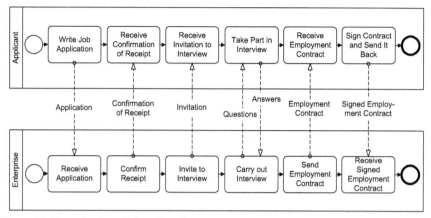

Figure 51: Example of a collaboration diagram

Therefore, each pool contains a complete process with a start event and an end event, with activities and the sequence flow. However, the two processes are not entirely independent, because messages are interchanged. As a part of the activity "Write Job Application", the applicant sends a message to the enterprise, containing his application. The enterprise takes this message in the activity "Receive Application". The following activity "Confirm Receipt" sends a message with a confirmation of receipt to the applicant.

On the applicant's side, the writing of an application is followed by the activity "Receive Confirmation of Receipt". This activity has an incoming message flow, i.e. it can only be completed when the message with the confirmation has been received.

As long as no confirmation of receipt has arrived, the applicant's process does not continue. This behavior is unfavorable because it may happen that an invitation to an interview arrives without a prior confirmation of receipt. The process cannot react to that invitation because it still waits for the confirmation of receipt. A better process would handle this possibility correctly, and also other alternatives, such as a rejection by the enterprise, would be considered. These cases have not been included in figure 51, to keep the model simple.

In the job posting process in chapter 2, the pool was labeled with the name of the process (figure 1). In figure 51, the labels do not contain the process names, but the partners' roles. This is typical for collaboration diagrams. In this example, both partners, applicant and enterprise, are displayed in the same way. The diagram could have been created both from the applicant's perspective and from the enterprise's perspective.

In practice, a collaboration diagram is often created by only one of the partners. In this case, the own pool can be labeled with the name of the process. The other pools are

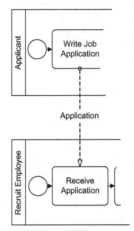

Figure 52: The company's own pool (bottom) is labeled with the name of the process

labeled with the partners' roles. In that way, it is clear which process is shown in the model, and also which partners are involved. If the above collaboration diagram is created by the enterprise, it may label its own pool with the process name "Recruit Employee" (figure 52).

Often, the own process is contained in an implicit pool which is not displayed in the diagram (cf. figure 53). A collaboration diagram may contain not more than one implicit pool.

5.2 Modeling Message Flows

A message flow can represent any kind of information exchange, for example a phone call or the sending of an e-mail, a fax, or a letter. Messages can also be connected to

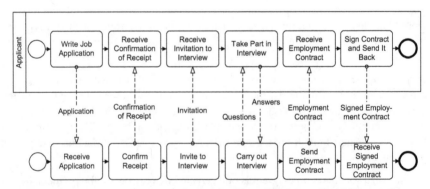

Figure 53: The company's own process is contained in an implicit pool which is not shown

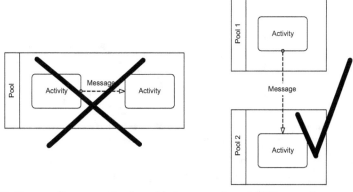

Figure 54: Message flows are only allowed between pools, not within a pool

physical objects, e.g. a delivery of goods can be modeled as a message flow in a collaboration. Of course, every kind of electronic data exchange can be shown as message flow, such as downloading a file or the call of another system's function, e.g. via a web service.

In contrast to the solid lines of the sequence flows, message flows are drawn with dashed lines. The start is marked with a little circle, the inside of the arrowhead is blank. In BPMN, message flows are only used for the communication of independent processes, which are in different pools. Thus, message flows are only allowed between different pools, but not within one pool (figure 54).

Sequence flows, on the other hand, are used for modeling the flow of an independent process within one pool. Therefore, sequence flows must not cross borders of pools (figure 55).

Lanes are subdivisions of pools. From the perspective of the BPMN specification, lanes rather provide supplementary information to a model, i.e. they do not influence the

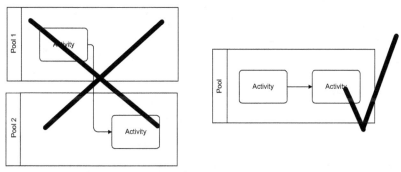

Figure 55: Sequence flows are only allowed within a pool, not between pools

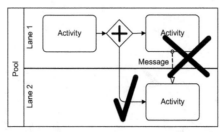

Figure 56: Sequence flows can cross the borders of lanes within a pool. The message flow on the right is still within one pool, and is therefore not allowed.

logic of the sequence flow. Therefore, sequence flows can cross the borders between lanes. Message flows between different lanes within the same pool are not allowed because start and end of a message flow must be in different pools (figure 56).

Correctly modeled message flows, i.e. message flows between different pools, can cross the borders between lanes without any problems. Examples are shown in figure 57.

5.3 Message Flows to Black Box Pools

The collaboration in figure 51 shows the internal processes of both involved partners. In many cases, however, only the internal processes of the own enterprise are known, but not the partner's processes. Only the messages are known which have to be exchanged with that partner during the process.

In such a case, this partner's pool is drawn without the process. The message flows then simply start and end at the borders of the pool (figure 58).

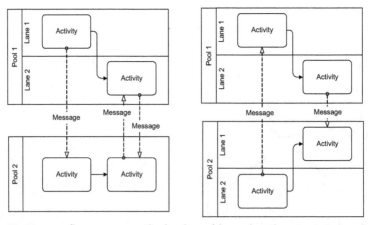

Figure 57: Message flows can cross the borders of lanes, but they must start and end in different pools

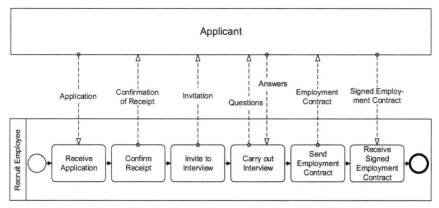

Figure 58: Message flow to a pool without modeling its internal details

If only the exchanged messages and their order are relevant, both pools can be drawn without their processes, as in figure 59. In that way, the exchange protocol of the collaboration can be documented. The partners need to agree on the content of this protocol so that the entire scenario will work. In this model, both pools are labeled with the names of the partners, since in contrast to figure 58 this model does not represent the specific view of one partner.

If an applicant asks the enterprise how a job application is handled, the content of figure 59 will be explained to him: First he needs to send an application; then he gets a confirmation of receipt, and so on. Thus, the message exchange protocol of the job application process represents the enterprise's interface to the applicant.

However, in that way no complex dependencies can be modeled regarding message exchange. It is not possible to model, for example, that after the confirmation of receipt, the applicant will either receive an invitation or a rejection. Nor can the fact be

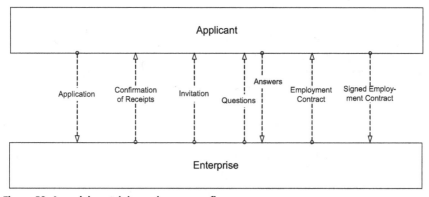

Figure 59: A model containing only message flows

expressed that the questions and answers of the interview will only be exchanged after an invitation has been sent. Such dependencies can be modeled in choreography diagrams (cf. chapter 11).

5.4 Private and Public Processes

In collaborations, it often makes sense not only to provide the partner with a black box representation of the own process but to disclose the process details as far as it is necessary for the co-operation. Thus, the partner can view the process and, for example, realize that a certain message is only sent under certain conditions.

A process may contain details which are not relevant to the partner, or which the company wants to keep secret. This can be achieved by providing a simplified view of the process to the partner. Such a simplified external view is also called "public process". Consequently, an internal process with all its details is called "private process".

Figure 60 shows an example of a private process. It presents in detail how an advertising agency produces an advertisement, and which messages it exchanges in doing so. This process contains a number of activities and loops which are not interesting to the customer, such as archiving, reviewing, and reworking.

The exchanged messages, on the other hand, are interesting for the customer. However, if the model contained only the pure message exchange without the process, the customer would not see, that after the feedback to the proof, another proof may be sent, for which feedback is required again, and so forth.

The public process in figure 61 does not present the details that are irrelevant for the customer. It only contains those activities that influence the collaboration. It is therefore the customer's view of the process from figure 60.

There are no defined rules for creating a public process out of a private process or vice versa. It is only required that the external behavior concerning the message exchange must be the same.

Typical actions during the transition from a private process to a public process include the combination of several elements into aggregated activities, as well as the removal of elements not required. In the above example, several elements have been removed from the public process: The two parallel loops for ensuring the quality of the text and the layout, as well as the activity "Archive Advertisement".

According to the BPMN 2.0 specification, an extended process "supports" a simpler process, if the entire process logic of the simple process is completely contained in the extended process. In this case, the simple (i.e. the supported) process can be replaced without any problems by the extended (i.e. the supporting) one. This is also true for private and public processes. The private process from figure 60 can be used instead of the public process from figure 61 without changing the externally visible process logic.

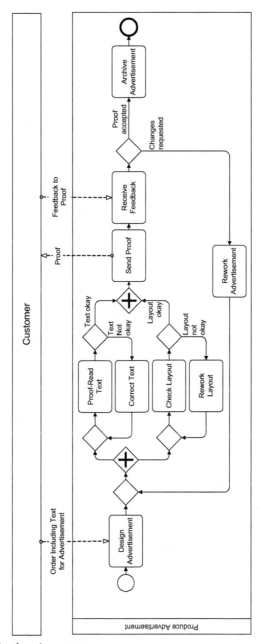

Figure 60: Example of a private process

53

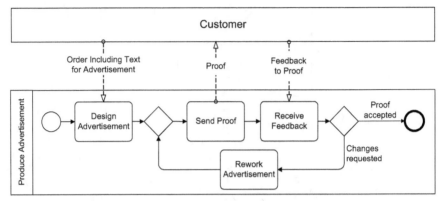

Figure 61: The public process related to the private process of figure 60

Concerning content, of course, there is a difference, because the resulting advertisement will be different, e.g. when the text is proof-read and corrected.

5.5 Multi-Instance Participants

In the previous examples, every pool represented exactly one participant. How can the interaction with a group of partners be modeled? If a company sends an inquiry to ten suppliers, it would be rather laborious to model ten pools. What is more, the exact number of partners is different in every process instance, and not yet known at modeling time.

In the example of hiring an employee (figure 51), the interaction of the enterprise with only one applicant was modeled. In practice, there are usually several applicants, one of whom is selected. Therefore, in figure 62 the applicant's pool is marked with three lines as a multi-instance participant. It stands for a group of applicants.

The messages are exchanged with each individual participant. For this, two loops have been included into the enterprise's process. In each cycle, the messages are exchanged with another applicant – until there is no applicant left. Each applicant's process is the same, shown in the pool on top.

Some interesting steps from the original hiring process are missing in the presented collaboration, especially the sending of the contract to the selected applicant. Consequently, the other applicants receive a rejection. The applicant's process then needs to react differently to different message flows. Either the signed contract is sent back, or the process is finished without further activities. Suitable modeling constructs for such a case are presented in the following chapter.

As shown in figure 63, the pool of a multi-instance participant can also be drawn as a black box.

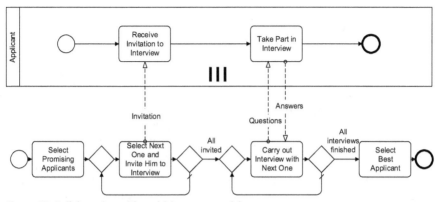

Figure 62: Collaboration with multi-instance participant

5.6 Use of Collaborations and Sequence Flows

It is obvious that collaboration diagrams are useful for modeling the interactions of several companies. However, pools need not necessarily represent companies. Instead, they can also stand for divisions or technical systems. A process that spans several units is usually modeled in one pool with several lanes, but it is also possible to model it with several pools. Each division then has its own pool, and the divisions' processes use message flows for communicating.

In which cases should a modeler use several distinct pools and message flows? Which cases, on the other hand, are better represented by a single pool with several lanes?

The deciding criterion for using a pool is, whether the process is defined or controlled entirely within that pool. For a process that is executed by a process engine of a work-flow or business process management system, this is easy to decide. The sequence that

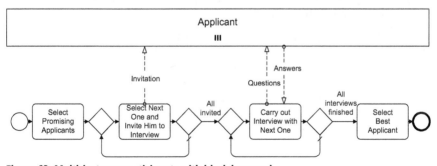

Figure 63: Multi-instance participants with black box pool

is controlled by the process engine should be within one pool. If the process interacts with another, separately controlled process, this other process is in another pool. The communication between them is modeled with message flows. Everything that is inside one pool is controlled by the process engine as a central unit.

Several different processes within one process engine are also shown in separate pools if they run in the form of separately controlled process instances which only communicate by exchanging data.

A process which is not – or only partially – executed by a process engine usually does not have such a central unit that controls every step in the process. However, for such a process it is still possible to identify a surrounding entity which provides a scope for defining and controlling the process, typically an enterprise or an organizational unit.

If a company defines processes that span several divisions, it is suitable to use one company pool with a lane for each division. On the other hand, there may be companies in which all divisions define their own independent processes, and they only agree on the information to be exchanged. In this case, it is also possible to model separate pools for the divisions, connected via message flows. However, this is inconsistent with the process management idea, according to which entire end-to-end processes should be analyzed and improved, rather than small processes within single divisions. If unchangeable interfaces between divisions are defined at the beginning, process improvements across divisional borders are almost completely prevented.

Within inter-company processes, each participating company usually retains the sovereignty of its own internal process. Therefore, using a collaboration diagram seems obvious.

On the other hand, there are also cases in which it makes sense to model an inter-company process completely with sequence flows inside one pool. In such a case, the pool represents the network of co-operating partners. This is reasonable when there is a very close co-operation, and the partners define the entire processes together. Examples for such close co-operations are the integration of suppliers in the automotive industry, enterprise consortia, and virtual enterprises. Since the partners work together in creating the process, they share the sovereignty over the process.

If the partners define their processes independently of each other, this may lead to the following situation. A supplier performs a quality control before shipping goods. When the customer receives the goods, he performs a quality control for the same goods again. If only the collaboration and each partner's individual process are analyzed, it cannot be detected that the same activity is performed twice. If the partners agree to jointly optimize the entire process, a model with one pool and sequence flows clearly shows the duplicate work. In the optimized process, only one partner performs the quality control. This, of course, is only possible if the customer can rely on the supplier.

In a second step, the partial processes of each partner need to be detailed and supported by information systems. For this step, modeling different pools and message flows may be appropriate again.

So there is no general answer to the question whether to use one pool with sequence flows, or several pools with message flows. For different situations and modeling purposes, this question will be answered differently.

5.7 Modeling Message Contents

Message flows carry content, such as documents, data sets or even physical objects. In the previous examples, the type of message content was indicated by the names of the message flows. However, BPMN distinguishes between the message flow and the message itself, i.e. the transmitted content. For business-oriented models, this differentiation is not that significant. For executable models, however, it may be important. The message flow involves the transmission and the receipt of defined messages. The message itself may contain a data structure, or the like, which may be stored or provided to a service.

Messages are displayed as envelope symbols (figure 64). There are blank envelope symbols, as well as shaded symbols. A shaded symbols usually stands for a message that is sent as an answer to a previous message. Blank symbols mark messages that initiate a message exchange. The benefit of these different colors becomes clear in the context of choreography diagrams (chapter 11). In a pure collaboration diagram, blank envelope symbols are sufficient. Alternatively, the message flows can be drawn entirely without envelopes. Modeling teams should decide for one style and use it consistently.

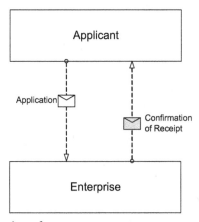

Figure 64: Use of envelope icons for message content

6   Events

An event is used to express that something has happened. It indicates a point in time. In contrast to an activity, it therefore does not have any duration. When modeling an event, two aspects are considered: The cause or trigger of the event, and its effect in the process.

Examples of typical triggers for events:

- A message arrives, such as an e-mail or a letter.

- A certain point in time is reached.
  Such an event and its effects are well-known to everyone whose alarm clock rings at a preset time.

- A certain time span ends.
  As opposed to an absolute point in time, the relative time span after another event or after the end of a preceding activity is considered. As an example, a kitchen timer is preset to a certain baking time when a cake is put into the oven. The timer's signal indicates the event "baking time completed". It is followed by other activities for preparing the cake.

- A condition becomes true.
  Such a condition could be "the outdoor temperature is at least 30°C". When reaching this temperature, it may be necessary to activate an air conditioner. Another example is the specification of "stop loss" limits for stock accounts. In order to avoid significant losses, a particular minimum price can be defined for each stock. If the stock price falls below this limit, the bank automatically sells this stock.

- An error occurs.
  For example, the outage of a system may require certain process steps in order to restore that system. Sometimes it is also necessary to find workarounds that enable important tasks to be performed without the system. Incoming orders may be temporarily recorded by hand. Later, when the outage is over, they are entered into the system.

  Further examples of errors may result from incomplete or inconsistent data, or a message that cannot be delivered.

The examples in the previous chapters already contained start and end events. However, events can also play a role within a process. Then they are modeled as intermediate events. Figure 65 shows the symbols of different event types: The start event is represented by a circle with a single line. The intermediate event's circle is drawn with two lines. In the end event's symbol, the space between the two lines is filled so that it has a thick border.

Figure 65: Types of events: start, intermediate, end

If required, the presented basic symbols can be complemented with icons for different kinds of triggers, such as messages or timers.

6.1 Example of the Use of Events

In figure 67, the different usages of events are shown using the example of a job application. This collaboration will be explained in several steps. The fragment in figure 66 shows the beginning of the process with a start event. The trigger of this event is not determined further. As a rule, such a process is started by a process participant, in this case, the applicant.

After the activity "Write Job Application", the intermediate event "Application sent" occurs. It is marked as a throwing message intermediate event, and it has an outgoing message flow "Application". This event is followed by another event, the catching message intermediate event "Confirmation received" with an incoming message flow "Confirmation of Receipt". This event only occurs when a confirmation of receipt actually has arrived. Until this moment, the process waits at this position, i.e. there is a token in front of the event. This token only moves on after the required message has been received.

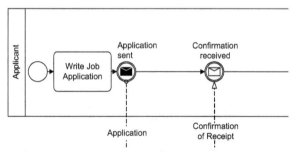

Figure 66: Start of the applicant's process (fragment from figure 67)

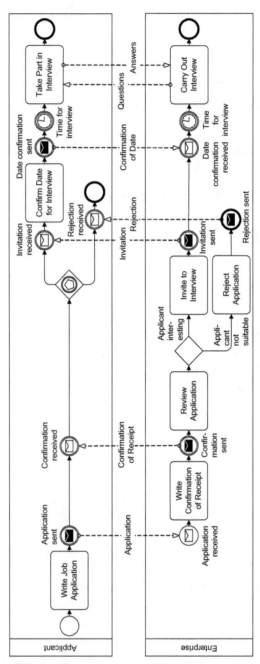

Figure 67: Example of the use of events

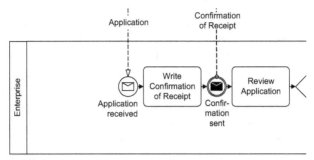

Figure 68: Start of the enterprise's process (fragment from figure 67)

What happens in this collaboration in the other partner's pool, i.e. in the enterprise? As the detail in figure 68 shows, the entire process is triggered by a catching message start event. Every time an application is received, a new process instance is created. In this instance, the first step is to write a confirmation of receipt. The intermediate event "Confirmation sent" follows. The process continues without interruption, and the activity "Review Application" is performed.

Sending the message "Confirmation of Receipt" has a direct effect on the applicant's process. In this process, the intermediate event "Confirmation received" has been waiting for this message. Now, the sequence flow in the applicant's process can be continued.

Here, the model has a disadvantage: If the applicant does not receive a confirmation of receipt, his process cannot be continued. If the enterprise would change its process and send an invitation to an interview without a previous confirmation of receipt, the applicant's process would not be able to handle it.

The second part of the enterprise's process is shown in figure 69. After "Review Application", the flow is split by an exclusive gateway. If the applicant is not suitable, the

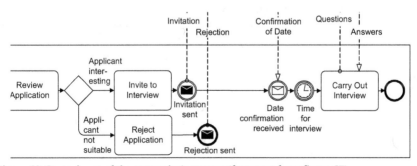

Figure 69: Second part of the enterprise's process (fragment from figure 67)

process finishes at the end event "Rejection sent". This is a throwing message event. Thus, when the process is finished, the message "Rejection" is sent.

If the applicant is interesting, however, he is invited to an interview. The message flow with the invitation triggers the intermediate event "Invitation sent". It is followed by the catching message intermediate event "Date confirmation received". Here, the process waits for a message.

At the next intermediate event, the timer event "Time for interview", the process waits again, until that time is reached. Then the activity "Carry out Interview" is performed. At this point, the process ends at an untyped end event. Unlike the event "Rejection sent", it only indicates the end of the process and does not send a message.

Since there is an exclusive gateway in figure 69, the enterprise either sends an invitation or a rejection. The applicant's process must react to these two alternatives. In the process fragment shown in figure 70, an event-based exclusive gateway is used for this.

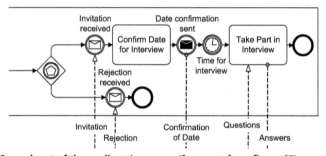

Figure 70: Second part of the applicant's process (fragment from figure 67)

At such a gateway, the intermediate event that occurs first determines the path to take. If a rejection is received first, the lower path is selected, and the process finishes at an untyped end event. However, if an invitation is received, the first event to occur is "Invitation received", and the upper path is selected. In this path, the interview date is confirmed which results in the throwing message intermediate event "Date confirmation sent". Then the applicant waits until it is time for the interview – just like the enterprise in its process. Finally, he takes part in the interview, and the process finishes at an untyped end event.

6.2   Start Events

The most common start event is probably the untyped event (without an icon in the circle). For this event type, the trigger is not exactly known, or it is not important. Often it can also be concluded from the context. The above-described job application process is most likely triggered by the applicant.

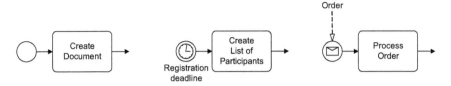

Figure 71: Types of start event triggers: None, timer, message

A start event is quite often triggered from the outside of the process. Workflow management systems usually display a list of processes which can be started by a user, depending on the user's role and rights. He selects the desired process from that list and starts it. By this, the start event is triggered within the process.

A process can also be a sub-process of another process (cf. chapter 7.1). As soon as the parent process activates the sub-process, the start event of the sub-process is automatically triggered.

Besides the untyped start event, especially timer start events and catching message start events are used in many BPMN models. When the registration deadline for a conference is reached, the conference organizers may start a process with further planning activities (figure 71, center). The processing of an order, on the other hand, is started when an order has been received (figure 71, right).

Figure 72 shows additional types of start events which are less frequently used. The conditional event (top, left) starts a process when the related condition becomes true. For example, a process for providing additional resources (e.g. employees or computing capacity) may be started when the utilization of the current resources exceeds 90%.

The start event at the top right is triggered by the reception of a signal. In contrast to a message which is always sent to a specific receiver, a signal is broadcasted everywhere.

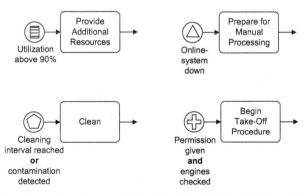

Figure 72: Further triggers for start events. Top: Conditional, signal. Bottom: Multiple, parallel multiple.

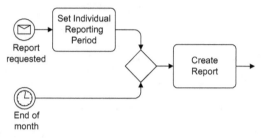

Figure 73: Several start events

The signal for starting a process may originate from the same pool, or from a different pool and another process. Such a signal could be sent for announcing that a certain computer system is not available ("Online-system down"). This might require a reaction of several processes to this signal. In the example shown above, a process is started for manually processing the data.

Finally, there are two symbols for start events with multiple triggers (figure 72, bottom). The multiple event is marked with a pentagon. It combines several events. If one of them occurs, the process is started. In the example shown, a cleaning activity is started when either the cleaning interval has been reached or a contamination has been detected. In contrast to this, in a parallel multiple event all of the combined events must have occurred. A take-off procedure can only be started as soon as the permission has been given and the engines have been checked. As long as only one of these two events has occurred, the process will wait for the second event, before commencing.

On the other hand, it is also possible to model several start events separately. In this case, the process is triggered when one of this events occur. The process in figure 73 starts when a request for a report is received, but also at the end of the month. If it is triggered by a request for a report, an individual reporting period is set, before a report is created. At the end of the month, however, the report is immediately created. Should both events happen to occur at the same time, still two independent process instances would be started.

In this case, it would not be possible to use a multiple start event instead of the two explicitly modeled events because the activity "Set Individual Reporting Period" is only performed when the process is started by one specific event. If both events would be followed directly by the gateway, instead, they could be replaced by a multiple start event, and the gateway would not be required.

If a process has several start events, not more than one of them should be an untyped event, i.e. a circle without an icon. If a process is started from the outside, e.g. by a process engine or a participant, the process starts at its untyped start event. If there are several of them, it is not clear at which of these untyped start events the process should commence.

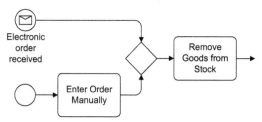

Figure 74: An untyped start event and a message start event as alternative triggers of a process

If there are several start events with a defined type (e.g. timer or message), it can always be determined which of them has occurred, and hence it is clear where the process starts.

If a process has both an untyped start event and one or more start events with specific types, it will be started at the untyped event if the process is triggered from outside. Alternatively, the occurrence of one of the other events (such as an incoming message) can also cause the start of the process. The process in figure 74 may be started from the outside, e.g. by a user who selects and activates the process in a workflow system. In this case, the process begins with the untyped start event, and the first activity is "Enter Order Manually". However, the process can also be started by the reception of an electronic order, and thus by the catching message start event.

It could be considered to use several untyped start events and to distinguish them by different names. However, BPMN does not specify any means for selecting an untyped event based on its name. Such a feature could be useful for connecting processes: A named end event of one process could automatically trigger another process's start event with the same name. Although such a connection via event names is not explicitly mentioned in the specification, there are examples of corresponding catching and throwing events which can easily be identified by a common name. Since BPMN does not rule out the use of several untyped start events, an individual modeling convention could be defined for connecting end events and start events via their names. On the other hand, other BPMN modelers may interpret such models in a different way, and modeling tools may not support this modeling convention.

In figure 75, the process "Introduce into New Position" should be started when "Recruit Employee" is finished, but also when "Job Change" is finished. The first activity to be performed depends on the preceding process. The connection is indicated by the names of the start events. The start events are annotated with the names of the preceding processes so that these can be found more easily.

It is not only possible to distinguish the different cases by using different untyped start events, but also by a single untyped start event, followed by an exclusive gateway (figure 76).

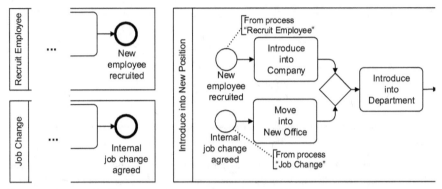

Figure 75: Connecting processes via start and end events with the same name

In both cases, the sequence of the processes must be modeled explicitly. They are connected as sub-processes in a higher-level process, as shown in figure 77. The plus sign means that there is a detailed process for this activity. Sub-processes are explained in chapter 7.

Sometimes it is suggested to connect processes via signal events or message flows. None of these solutions, however, is perfect. A signal is not only sent to a specific process, but it is broadcasted to all processes. This is not intended here because only one subsequent process should be started. In this respect, a message flow should be preferred, because a message flow runs to one specific process. However, this would imply that the two processes are independent of each other, not being sub-processes of an overall end-to-end process.

If a start event has more than one outgoing sequence flows, all of them are activated when the process starts, i.e. they behave as parallel flows.

It is also possible to model processes entirely without start events. In this case, every activity without incoming sequence flow has an implicit start event.

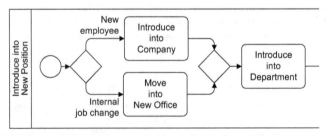

Figure 76: Use of an exclusive gateway as an alternative to figure 75

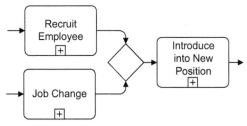

Figure 77: A higher level process connecting the different processes

When such a process is started, all these activities with implicit start events are activated in parallel. In figure 78, at the beginning, a computer and software are acquired in parallel. The two resulting tokens are joined in the parallel gateway before the computer is set up. The model fragment in figure 78 is, therefore, equivalent to the one in figure 79. Here, only one token is created by the explicit start event. This token is duplicated at the splitting parallel gateway so that the activities "Acquire Computer" and "Acquire Software" are also performed in parallel.

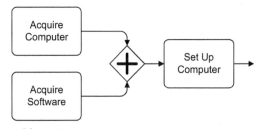

Figure 78: A process without start events

Other elements which usually have an incoming sequence flow also contain an implicit start event, if the incoming sequence flow is missing. As an example, the splitting gateway in figure 80 contains such an implicit start event.

A modeler must decide whether to use implicit or explicit start events. If there is at least one explicit start event in a process, there must not be any activities or gateways without incoming sequence flow. In most cases it is advisable to use explicit start events.

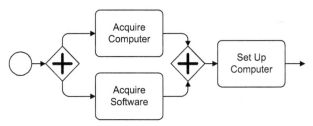

Figure 79: The process from figure 78 with an explicit start event

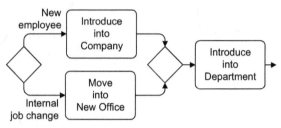

Figure 80: Gateways can also have implicit start events

6.3   End Events

An end event is displayed with a thick border, as already mentioned. Besides the untyped end event, which simply removes an incoming token (figure 81, left), there are also special types of end events. In the center of figure 81, there is an end event that not only consumes an incoming token but also sends a message.

In contrast to the catching message start event, the envelope symbol of the throwing message end event is filled. This principle is also valid for other types of events: The symbols of throwing events are always filled, the corresponding catching events contain the same symbols, but they are blank.

The end event on the right is a terminate event. Like an untyped end event, it deletes a token when it arrives. However, it not only deletes this single token but it also terminates the entire process, i.e. any other tokens in the entire process are also removed at the same time.

The benefit of this event becomes clear when looking at a process with several end events. On the one hand, these end events can be exclusive. In figure 82, an application is either sent by post or by e-mail. Hence, only one of the two end events can be reached. If one of these end events has occurred, the entire process is finished, because there is not any remaining token left.

In figure 83, on the other hand, the two activities "Create Graphics" and "Write Text" are performed in parallel. The start event creates a token, and the parallel gateway duplicates it. Each of the two resulting tokens flows through one of the two parallel paths. Therefore, both end events occur. Each of them deletes one token.

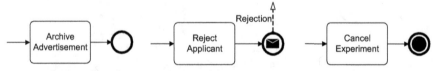

Figure 81: Types of end event results: None, message, terminate

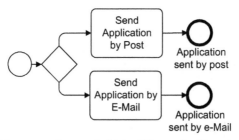

Figure 82: Several end events, only one of which will be reached in a single process instance

Both activities do not necessarily run simultaneously, and they may have different durations. Thus, the two end events usually occur one after the other. If the end event "Graphics created" occurs first, it deletes one token. The process is not yet finished since there is still the second token on its way. Only when the last token has been deleted, the entire process is finished.

In both cases, it would have been possible to use only one common end event for both sequence flows, since an end event simply removes any arriving token.

In some cases, however, it is desired to terminate the entire process as soon as one end event is reached. An example can be found in figure 84. Here, again, the parallel gateway emits two tokens via the parallel sequence flows. The skills and experiences of a job applicant are checked, and his formal qualification is checked in parallel, too. If the results of both checks are positive, the two tokens flow through the exclusive gateways to the joining parallel gateway. Here they are joined to one token which eventually reaches the untyped end event "Application accepted".

If one of the checks has a negative result, the respective token flows through the other exit of the exclusive gateway to the end event "Application rejected". Since it is a terminate event, the other token is also deleted, and the process is immediately finished.

In the case of one negative result, the result of the other check is irrelevant, because the application will be rejected in any event. Thus, the process can be terminated immediately.

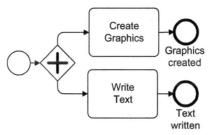

Figure 83: Several end events, which will all be reached in a single process instance

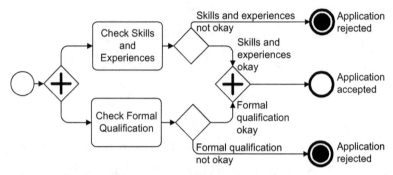

Figure 84: A terminate end event immediately finishes the entire process

If untyped end events were used, the other token would still move on. If for example, the skills and experiences are not sufficient, and the check of the formal qualification has not been carried out yet, this second activity will not even need to be started. This is achieved by the terminate event which deletes the second token, as well.

Replacing the terminate end events by untyped end events would cause a problem if the result of one of the checks is positive and the other negative. The token coming from the negative check would reach the end event "Application rejected". The token from the positive check, on the other hand, would flow to the joining parallel gateway. Since the second token already has been deleted and cannot arrive anymore, the token would be stuck at the parallel gateway, and the process could not be finished. This problem is avoided by using terminate events.

Further types of end events are the throwing of a signal and the multiple end event (figure 85). As already mentioned, signals do not have a specific receiver, they can be received anywhere in the same process, as well as in other processes. In the presented example, the event sends the signal that a new software version has been released. Different processes can react to that signal, e.g. the sales process or a process for installing new software. For the software releasing process, however, it is not relevant which other processes need that information. Therefore, a signal is sent to everyone.

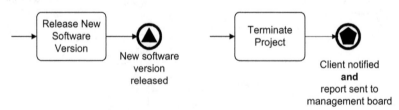

Figure 85: Further types of end event results: Signal and multiple

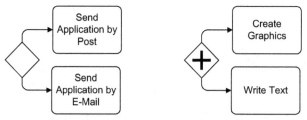

Figure 86: Activities without outgoing sequence flows have implicit end events

A multiple end event is used when the end of a process has several consequences. When the end event is reached, all the combined partial events occur. In the example, several messages are sent.

Just like start events, explicit end events can also be omitted. In this case, all activities and gateways without outgoing sequence flows have implicit end events. These have the same behavior as normal untyped end events. The models from figure 82 and 83 can also be modeled as in figure 86.

For implicit end events the same rule is valid as for implicit start events: A process may either have only implicit or only explicit end events. A mixture of both is not allowed. This also applies to start and end events: If there are explicit start events in a process, the end events must be explicit, as well. Accordingly, implicit start events require implicit end events and vice versa.

In chapters 8 and 9, further types of end events will be introduced which are required for sub-processes and for modeling compensations and transactions.

6.4 Intermediate Events

An intermediate event can be used at any arbitrary position within a process. It has an incoming and an outgoing sequence flow. Its symbol is a circle with a double-line border.

Usually, intermediate events are only modeled when

1. an event that is relevant to others is triggered within a process (e.g. a message or a signal is sent), or
2. there is a reaction to an event within a process (e.g. when a message is received or a certain point in time is reached).

Start events can only be "catching", i.e. they can receive something or react to a trigger. End events, on the other hand, can only be "throwing", i.e. they can send or trigger something. In contrast to this, intermediate events can either be catching or throwing events.

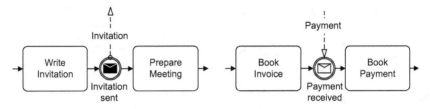

Figure 87: Message intermediate events: Throwing (left) and catching (right)

Figure 87 shows examples of a catching and a throwing intermediate event. The throwing message intermediate event contains a filled envelope symbol. In this example, the intermediate event "Invitation sent" is triggered by the completion of the preceding activity "Write Invitation". When this event occurs, the message "Invitation" is sent. At the same time, the sequence flow is continued, and the following activity "Prepare Meeting" is triggered.

It would also be possible to omit the intermediate event. The message flow would then originate directly from the activity "Write Invitation". When the sending of the message is modeled as an event between the two activities, it becomes clear that the message is sent when the preceding activity is completed, rather than at an arbitrary point in time during the execution of "Write Invitation".

The catching message intermediate event is represented by a blank envelope symbol (figure 87, right). It reacts to a message that arrives via the incoming message flow. When the activity "Book Invoice" is finished, a token flows to the intermediate event "Payment received". Here it waits for the reception of the message "Payment". As long as the payment is not received, the token remains at this position. The intermediate event only occurs when the payment arrives. Then the token flows on and triggers the activity "Book Payment".

Of course, the received payment must be related to the invoice that has been sent by the same process instance. Since there are many instances of this process in parallel, many different invoices have been sent, and many payments are received. These payments need to be assigned to the related process instances. If this is done by a person, he will identify the correct invoice based on the invoice number that is referred to in the payment information.

If a process engine automatically assigns a received message to the related process instance, this is called "correlation".

Figure 88 shows a timer intermediate event with a clock symbol. After a token arrives at such an event, it waits until a definite time. Typically it is not a previously determined absolute point in time, but the end of a certain time span. In figure 88, a cake is put into the oven. The activity "Take out Cake" starts after waiting for one hour.

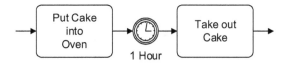

Figure 88: Timer intermediate event

A condition becoming true can trigger an intermediate event, too. In figure 89, first the oven is turned on. The process then waits until the temperature exceeds 180°C before the cake is put into the oven.

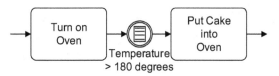

Figure 89: Conditional intermediate event

Intermediate events can also send and receive signals. This is indicated by a filled triangle or a blank triangle, respectively. In the top process in figure 90, a throwing intermediate event signals that a new software version is available. After that, the process continues without interruption with the activity "Inventory New Version of Software". In the process at the bottom, a defective software application is shut down. Then the process waits for the signal "New version of software available". Only when this signal arrives, the activity "Download and Install New Version" can be carried out.

Sometimes it is necessary to split a large model to several pages. In this case, it is helpful to use links to other pages. They enable the user to follow the sequence flow when it is continued on another page. Such off-page connectors are represented by "link" intermediate events. They are marked with arrows.

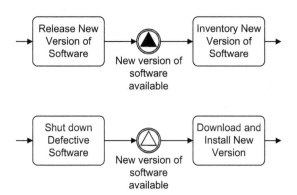

Figure 90: Signal intermediate event: Throwing (top) and catching (bottom)

73

Figure 91: Link intermediate event connecting to another page

Figure 91 shows an outgoing link "A" at the end of a page. It refers to the incoming link of the same name on the next page. This means that a sequence flow runs from Activity X to Activity Y.

It is also possible to model a link to another position on the same page. This is especially useful for replacing a long sequence flow connection around many other model elements. The model becomes clearer when such a long connection is replaced by a throwing and a catching link event.

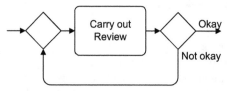

Figure 92: Normal loop

The backward looping sequence flow from figure 92 can also be drawn as in figure 93. Here, the sequence flow is forwarded from the right, outgoing link "B" to the left, incoming link "B".

Intermediate events can also be marked with a multiple symbol if there are several alternative triggers or several consequences of the event. Again, there are catching and throwing events. The latter has a filled symbol (figure 94). The catching version of this event is used for modeling that a token needs to wait at this position until one of the partial events has occurred. At the throwing multiple intermediate event, all of the combined consequences occur at the same time, as it is already known from the throwing multiple end event.

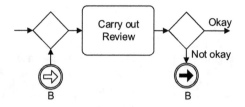

Figure 93: Modeling a loop with incoming and outgoing links

74

Figure 94: Multiple intermediate event (catching and throwing)

There is also a parallel multiple intermediate event (figure 95). In contrast to a normal multiple event, *all* combined events (e.g. the reception of several different messages) must have occurred, before a waiting token is moved on.

Figure 95: Parallel multiple intermediate event

Finally, there is also the untyped version of the intermediate event, without a symbol inside the double-bordered circle. Other than start and end events, untyped intermediate events are rarely used. In principle, it is possible to model simply that a certain state has been reached within a process. The event "Order entered" in figure 96 indicates that the order that is being processed has changed its state to "entered". In this example, this information is rather trivial. What is more, the untyped intermediate event does neither have any effect on this process nor on other processes. Therefore, this event is normally not modeled.

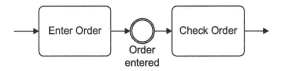

Figure 96: Untyped intermediate event

Occasionally, however, it does make sense to model such untyped events. Sometimes it is useful to analyze the different possible states of an object. This can be done with a UML statechart diagram, for example. With untyped intermediate events, it can then be modeled where each state is reached in a process.

Figure 97 contains the different states of a document. The events always indicate the entry into a new state. In contrast to an event without duration, a state lasts some time. A different way of representing states of data objects will be shown in chapter 10.

How does an intermediate event handle multiple incoming or outgoing sequence flows? In the case of multiple incoming sequence flows, each arriving token is handled separately, i.e. the event does not wait for additional tokens. Several outgoing sequence flows are treated as parallel flow, i.e. for each outgoing sequence flow, a token is emitted.

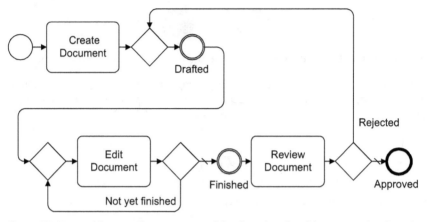

Figure 97: Untyped intermediate events used for denoting the object states that have been reached

6.5 Event-Based Decisions

In chapter 3.1, exclusive gateways have been discussed. Such a gateway selects exactly one out of several sequence flows. The presented gateways are data-based gateways, i.e. the decision is made on the basis of provided data.

Figure 98 shows an example that has already been presented. Here, the value of a data element "distance" is used for evaluating the conditions at the sequence flows. If this value is greater than 500 km, the upper path is selected, otherwise the bottom path. Such kinds of data are relevant for the control flow, but they need not to be modeled in BPMN (although modeling of data objects is possible, as shown in chapter 10). It is always assumed that within a process it is possible to access all data from everywhere.

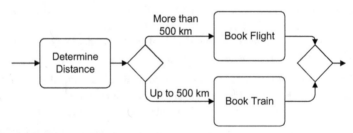

Figure 98: Data-based decision

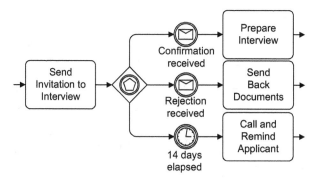

Figure 99: Event-based decision

BPMN provides a second type of exclusive gateway, the event-based gateway. This gateway also selects one of several paths, but the decision is based on which event occurs. In figure 99, an invitation to an interview is sent. At the gateway, one of the three outgoing sequence flows is selected. In each of these sequence flows, the next element is a catching intermediate event. The event that occurs first decides which path to take.

If a confirmation is received, the interview is prepared. If a rejection is received, the documents are sent back. If, however, 14 days have elapsed without one of the other two events occurring, the applicant is called and reminded. Only that event is considered that occurs first. If the event "Confirmation received" occurs within 14 days, the event "14 days elapsed" does not have any effect anymore.

In contrast to a data-based exclusive gateway, the exits of an event-based exclusive gateway have no conditions. Instead, the first element in each outgoing sequence flow must be a catching intermediate event. This is required for selecting a sequence flow.

In the case of a catching message intermediate event, however, BPMN also provides another possibility. Since messages can also be received by activities, such an event can also be replaced by an activity. It must be an activity that does nothing else but receive the message. Otherwise, if the message were received later during the activity, the activity would have to be triggered before it is known whether the related message arrives first. An activity that only receives a message is classified as a "receive" activity (cf. chapter 7.4). It is marked with an envelope symbol in the upper left corner. The model fragment from figure 99 thus can be modeled as in figure 100. However, the logic of the decision is more clearly visible if events are used.

Sequence flows which have been split by an event-based exclusive gateway can be merged by an ordinary exclusive gateway. At a split it does not matter whether the selection of a sequence flow was based on data or events. It is only important that every time a token arrives only via exactly one sequence flow. In principle, the merge

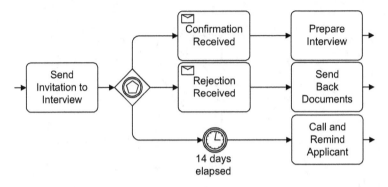

Figure 100: Event-based decision with message-receiving activities

could also be expressed by an event-based exclusive gateway symbol, but the logic is exactly the same as that of a normal merging exclusive gateway.

In chapter 6.2 a process has been modeled that can be started in different ways. These were represented by several start events. Sometimes this is alternatively modeled as in figure 101. Since the event-based gateway does not have an incoming sequence flow, it contains an implicit start event. Thus, the process starts and immediately waits for the first intermediate event. In fact, the process is started by the intermediate event. When using this kind of modeling, the use of several start events is avoided. Models with more than one start events may lead to misinterpretations. The meaning of the model in figure 101 is the same as in figure 73.

There is another alternative for starting a process: The event-based parallel gateway. Here, all events after the gateway must occur at the beginning. The first event causes a process instance to be created. After that, the process waits for the other events before it is continued. The same behavior can also be modeled with a parallel multiple start event. The model in figure 102 is, therefore, equivalent to the one in the lower right corner of figure 72.

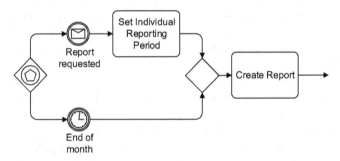

Figure 101: Event-based gateway for starting a process

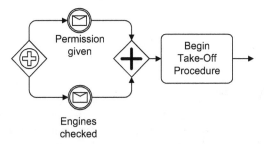

Figure 102: Event-based parallel gateway for starting a process

There is no event-based parallel gateway to be used after the start of the process. If a process needs to wait for several events which can occur in any order, normal parallel gateways can be used for splitting the sequence flow before these events, as well as for the merge after the events.

7 Activities

7.1 Sub-Processes

BPMN models can contain two types of activities: Tasks and sub-processes. Tasks are not subdivided. Sub-processes, on the other hand, contain other detailed processes.

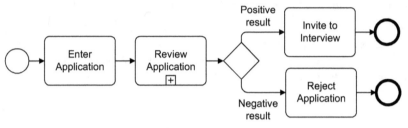

Figure 103: Process with sub-process "Review Application"

The process in figure 103 comprises the three tasks "Enter Application", "Invite to Interview", "Reject Application", and the Sub-Process "Review Application". The latter is marked with a little "+"-Symbol. The fact that "Enter Application" is a task does not mean that it cannot be further subdivided, but simply that this has not been done in this model.

Figure 104 shows the details of the sub-process "Review Application". When in the parent process a token arrives at this activity, the sub-process's start event is triggered, i.e. it creates a token. The token flows through the sub-process just like through any other normal process. At some point it reaches one of the two end events. By this, the sub-process is finished, and in the parent process a token is emitted to the outgoing sequence flow.

In the parent process, it does not matter which of the two events has been reached. It is only required that the sub-process has been finished completely before a token is passed on.

In the example, however, it is important with regard to contents which end event has been reached because the following gateway distinguishes whether the result of the review has been positive or negative. However, according to the BPMN syntax, there is no relation between the different end events within a sub-process and the conditions at the decision in the higher-level process.

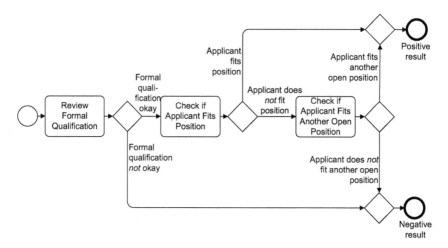

Figure 104: Sub-process "Review Application"

These models rather have to be interpreted in the following way. The sub-process creates data which contain the review result. These data are then available in the parent process. They will be evaluated by the gateway conditions. As already mentioned it is always assumed that all data within a process are available everywhere. This is also true for embedded sub-processes.

The parent process in the example could have an attribute "result" which can receive the values "positive" or "negative". The annotations in figure 105 describe for each activity which value is assigned to this attribute. The conditions at the gateway in fi-

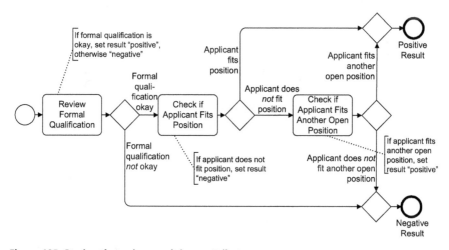

Figure 105: Storing the review result in an attribute

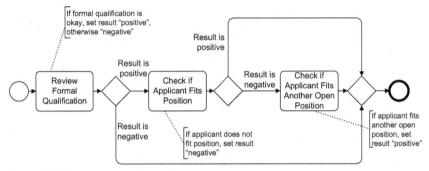

Figure 106: Alternative modeling of the sub-process

gure 103 simply evaluate the attribute value for making the decision. The conditions at the gateways in the sub-process can also make use of the result attribute.

The proposed mechanism for transmitting a sub-process's results to a parent process is independent from the end events. Therefore, the sub-process could also be modeled as in figure 106. Here, the token always reaches the only end event, and the review result is again passed by an attribute.

The structure of figure 104, however, is more expressive and easier to understand – especially if cumbersome annotations should be avoided. Therefore, it may be a good idea to specify as a modeling convention that the reaction to different sub-process end events should be modeled as described above.

If the process is carried out manually, there is no process engine to manage an attribute "result". Either the result is forwarded by an involved person, or it is noted on a form accompanying the process. The principle is not changed by this manual information transfer.

For a sub-process it is also possible to have several end events which are all reached via parallel paths. In this case, the sub-process is only finished when all tokens in the sub-process have been swallowed by end events.

If a sub-process is finished, one token will be emitted to each of the sub-process's outgoing sequence flows. In the case of a conditional flow, a token will only be emitted if the conditions are true.

It should be taken care that a sub-process does not have more than one untyped start event. Otherwise, it is not clear where the sub-process starts after having been triggered by the parent process.

Besides using separate diagrams for sub-processes, it is also possible to insert the details of the sub-process directly into the model of the parent process. For this, the sub-process is positioned inside the enlarged activity symbol (figure 107).

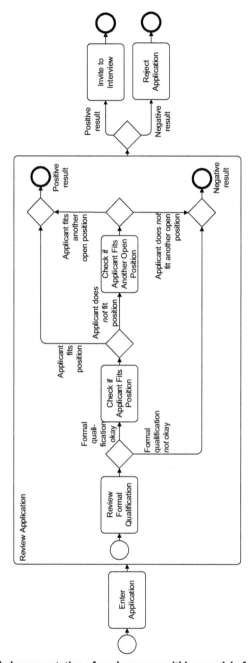

Figure 107: Expanded representation of a sub-process within a model of the parent process

Some modeling tools also allow for expanding and collapsing sub-processes, so that the context of the entire process remains visible, and the details of a sub-process can be viewed when desired. The expanded view of sub-processes is only reasonable up to a certain model size. Otherwise, the diagrams get too large and complex, and it is difficult to understand them.

Sub-processes can contain other sub-processes so that hierarchical process models can be created, consisting of any number of levels.

Like top-level processes, sub-processes can also have implicit start events and end events (cf. chapters 6.2 and 6.3). In figure 108, all three tasks are activated in parallel when the sub-process is started. As soon as all three tasks are finished, the sub-process is also finished, and a token flows from the sub-process to the end event of the parent process.

It has already been explained that the start and end events of a process must all be either explicit or implicit. A combination of explicit and implicit events is not allowed. Since every sub-process is a process of its own, the usage of explicit or implicit events can be different to that of the parent process. Therefore, the diagram in figure 108 is correct. The parent process has only explicit start and end events; the sub-process has only implicit events.

In figure 108 the three tasks in the sub-process are executed in parallel. Therefore, the same logic could also be modeled with parallel gateways, as in figure 109.

It could be argued that the modeled contents in both figures have to be slightly different. Tasks 2, 3 and 4 are parts of a sub-process, i.e. they are on a more detailed modeling level. Therefore, it could be assumed that these tasks are more detailed tasks than Task 1. In the example with parallel gateways, all activities are on the same level and, therefore, they should have the same level of detail.

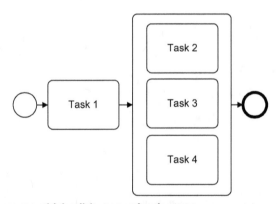

Figure 108: Sub-process with implicit start and end events

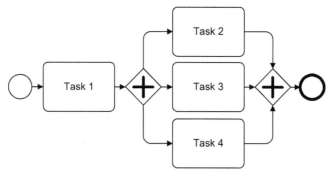

Figure 109: Modeling the process from figure 108 with parallel gateways

This argument is true if sub-processes are used for creating model hierarchies – from a high-level overview model to very detailed process models. However, in BPMN sub-processes are not only used for this purpose, but also for grouping several activities within a loop (cf. chapter 7.2), or for creating a scope that can be interrupted as a whole (cf. chapters 8 and 9). In these cases, the activities in a sub-process have the same level of detail as the activities of the parent process. Therefore, the sub-process in figure 108 may only be a grouping of activities, which even may have been created for achieving a more compact diagram than with parallel gateways. It is interesting that the BPMN specification states that the main reason for introducing implicit start and end events actually was this more compact way of modeling parallel activities [OMG 2013, p. 172].

7.2 Loops and Multi-Instance Activities

Many activities are repeated several times in a process. This can be modeled with loops. In figure 110, a purchase for all employees is to be made (e.g. for newly designed business cards). In the beginning, the demand is identified. Since not all employees may be reached at once, this task is repeated until all employees have reported their demands. After that, an offer is obtained. If the offer is not satisfying, another offer is obtained. "Obtaining offer" is repeated until finally a suitable offer has been found. Only then the flow continues with "Place Order".

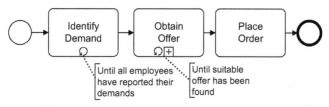

Figure 110: Loop activities

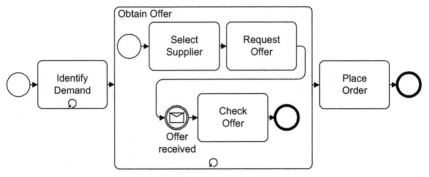

Figure 111: Expanded sub-process for a loop activity

A loop activity has a small circle-shaped arrow at the bottom. Sub-processes can also be marked as loops, both in the collapsed and in the expanded form. Figure 111 shows the process with the expanded loop sub-process.

Without any further information, a loop would be repeated endlessly. Therefore, it must be defined how often the loop should be repeated. This can be done with an exit condition. The loop is repeated continuously until the exit condition is true. In figure 110, the exit conditions are displayed as informal text annotations. For example, the activity "Identify Demand" is repeated until the condition "All employees have reported their demands" becomes true.

Instead of an exit condition, it is also possible to define a condition for the continuation of the loop. In this case, the loop activity is repeated as long as the condition is true. Only when it is no longer true, the loop is terminated.

For an automated process which is executed by a process engine, such conditions need to be defined in a specific formal language which can be processed by the engine. BPMN provides attributes for storing such conditions. The specification proposes the XML query language XPath for specifying such conditions, but it explicitly allows other languages, as well. In most cases it depends on the process engine which formal language is used.

The definition of a loop may additionally include the minimum and the maximum number of repetitions. The modeler can also specify whether the condition should be evaluated before or after the loop is performed. If it is evaluated before each loop cycle, the exit condition may already be true at the beginning, and the loop will not be performed at all. If it is evaluated after each looping, the loop is performed at least once.

For process models which will not be automated, it is recommended to use annotations. The conditions should be written as easily understandable textual statements.

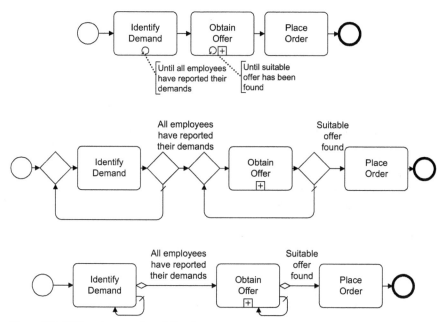

Figure 112: Different ways of modeling loops

Loops can also be modeled in an entirely different way. A splitting exclusive gateway is placed behind the activity which should be repeated. One of the sequence flows runs back to a merging gateway in front of the activity. Figure 112 shows different representations of loops: With loop activities (top) and with backward running sequence flows, modeled with gateways (center) and with conditional sequence flows (bottom).

It is a matter of modeling style which of these alternatives is used. In business-level models, the backward running sequence flows are often used, because the loops become more clearly visible. For automated processes loop activities are preferred, because they are easier to handle. When using sequence flows for modeling loops, very complex, nested cycles may be created. These are very prone to modeling errors which may result in deadlocks.

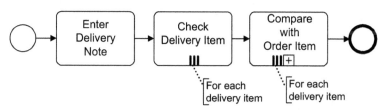

Figure 113: Multi-instance activities

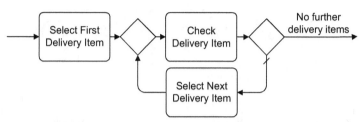

Figure 114: Modeling of the activity "Check Delivery Item" without a multi-instance activity

Another special kind of activity is the multi-instance activity. It is marked with three parallel lines at the bottom (cf. figure 113). It is used for dealing with an entire collection of objects that need to be processed. The multi-instance activity is carried out several times, once for each object of the collection.

The process in figure 113 starts with entering a delivery note. Such a delivery note usually contains several delivery items. The activity "Check Delivery Item" has to be carried out for each of these delivery items. Thus, the number of repetitions is determined by the number of delivery items. In the next step, each delivery item is compared with the corresponding order item. Therefore, the sub-process "Compare with Order Item" is also a multi-instance activity.

Multi-instance activities have attributes for specifying the elements to be processed. If formal statements are not needed, annotations can be used again, as in figure 113.

In principle, it is also possible to model the same behavior with loops (loop activities or backward running sequence flows). This is shown for the activity "Check Delivery Item" in figure 114. However, if a multi-instance activity is used, the rather trivial support tasks "Select First Delivery Item" and "Select Next Delivery Item" can be omitted.

A multi-instance activity is also different from a loop activity. For a multi-instance activity, the number of repetitions is known in advance since this is determined by the size of the collection of objects. For a loop activity, however, the exit conditions need to be tested after each repetition. Therefore, the number of repetitions does not need to be known in advance. In many cases, the exact number only turns out during the execution of the loop.

In contrast to loop activities, multi-instance activities do not necessarily need to be repeated sequentially in a certain order. The different objects can be processed in any order, and also in parallel. If a sequential processing is required, the three lines of the multiple marker are drawn horizontally.

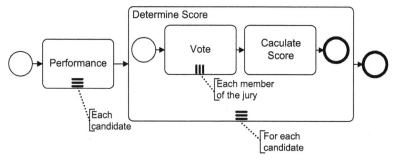

Figure 115: Sequential and parallel multi-instance activities

Figure 115 illustrates this with a process of a talent show on television. First, each candidate delivers a performance. The group of candidates is known in advance. A loop activity would not be the right choice for this because then after each performance it would have to be checked whether there is still another candidate who wants to perform. On the other hand, the performances must not be in parallel, because audience and jury want to watch all performances. "Performance" is thus marked as a sequential multi-instance activity.

After the last performance, the sub-process "Determine Score" is started. This sub-process is also repeated sequentially for each candidate. Within the sub-process, there is another multiple-instance activity: "Vote" is executed for every jury member. In this example, they vote in parallel.

Like in the case of the parallel gateway, "parallel" does not necessarily mean "simultaneously". There is just no sequence defined. Before "Calculate Score" can be started, all votes must have been submitted.

7.3 Ad-hoc Sub-Processes

An ad-hoc sub-process is marked with a tilde. Although the activities contained in such a sub-process are determined, the order is not known in advance, because it will only emerge when the sub-process is carried out. Typical examples are creative, knowledge-intensive processes. Which activity should be performed at what time is flexibly decided by the personnel, based on the current situation. Repetitions and parallel processing are also possible.

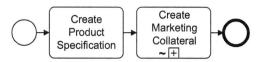

Figure 116: Ad-hoc sub-process

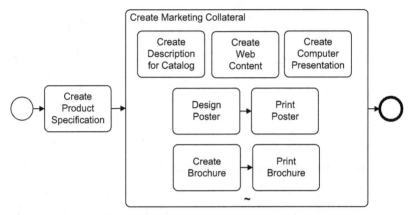

Figure 117: Expanded ad-hoc sub-process

Figure 116 contains the ad-hoc sub-process "Create Marketing Collateral". The expanded presentation in figure 117 shows the activities which have to be carried out. Since for the most activities, the sequence is not known in advance, no sequence flow can be shown for them. At those places where a certain order needs to be followed, a sequence flow can also be drawn within an ad-hoc sub-process. For example, the activity "Print Poster" can only be carried out when the poster has been designed. Therefore, a sequence flow was inserted between these two activities. The same is true for the activities "Create Brochure" and "Print Brochure".

The tilde as ad-hoc marker can only be used for sub-processes, but not for tasks.

7.4 Types of Tasks

The tasks carried out in a process can be divided into different types. The BPMN specification defines the following types that strongly reflect the view of process automation with process engines:

- Service Task
  A service task is an automated function, e.g. the call of an application function or a web service.

- Receive Task
  A receive task receives a message. It corresponds to a catching message event.

- Send Task
  A send task sends a message. It corresponds to a throwing message event.

- User Task
  A user task expects input from a user. This is a typical task type within a so-called "Human interaction workflow". A user receives his due tasks in a task

list from which he can select the task he wants to work on. The actual work is done by entering information into a user interface dialog.

- Business Rule Task
  In a business rule task, one or more business rules are applied to produce a result or to make a decision. It is common to use a business rule management system which is called by the process engine. The business rules management system then evaluates the rules that apply to the current situation.

- Script Task
  A script contains statements which are processed directly by the process engine.

- Manual Task
  A manual task is carried out without IT support.

- Abstract Task
  No type has been defined.

Except for the abstract task, the different tasks are marked with icons (figure 118).

Modelers are allowed to define additional task types and mark them with their own icons in the task symbol. However, this is not supported by every BPMN modeling tool.

7.5 Calling Processes and Global Tasks

Until now two types of activities have been used: Sub-processes and tasks. Tasks are not decomposed any further. Normal sub-processes and tasks are part of the process they belong to. This means they depend on the process and cannot be used separately.

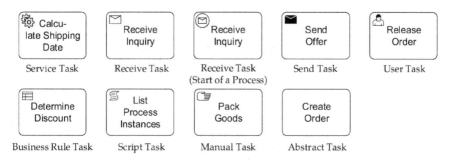

Figure 118: Icons for different types of tasks

In many cases, however, an activity should be re-used in several processes. BPMN provides the construct of the "call activity" for this. When a call activity appears in a process, the actual activity is defined at another place, and it will only be called from the process.

If the called activity is a task, a so-called global task will be called. A global task is defined only once, i.e. its attribute values, such as the name, the description, involved functions or web services, parameters, etc. exist only once. This task can then be called within different processes. The attributes of a global task are not defined in a graphical model, but – depending on the modeling tool – in an attribute dialog which can be opened for a call activity element.

As shown in figure 119, a call activity is drawn with a thick border. In this case, "Determine Discount" is defined as a global task. Process 1 and Process 2 each contain a call activity referring to this global task. A business rule task is used in this example. Global tasks can be of any task type, and also without a specific type.

Especially for automated processes, there is an important distinction between normal embedded activities and call activities. Normal activities automatically have access to any information within the process. In the example above, there could be two variables for storing the total amounts of the offer and the order. In a normal activity, such as "Create Invoice", these values can be directly accessed and used. If variables are defined in a process, they will be visible in all tasks and sub-processes of that process – except in call activities.

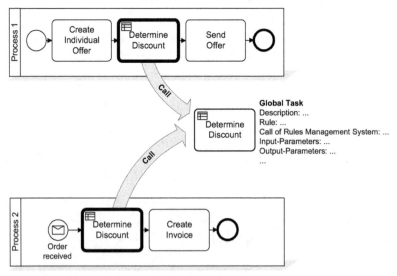

Figure 119: Call of a global task from different processes

Since the activity "Determine Discount" has been defined as a global task, it cannot access the value of such a process variable. This is because the global task can be called from different processes. It is therefore required to be independent from the calling process. For exchanging information between a calling process and a called global task, interfaces must be defined. An interface determines input and output parameters. BPMN also provides constructs for parameters, but they are not graphically displayed in models.

Although the visibility of variables is rather a subject of executable process models, it should also be considered for business-oriented models whether an activity can be used more than once. In the following chapter 7.6, a business example will be presented which illustrates a sub-process's dependency from the surrounding process.

A call activity can also call another process. In figure 120, the process "Put Goods into Stock" is called from two other processes. The "+"-marker indicates that the called activity is a process. This called process, "Put Goods into Stock", itself is a normal process. It could also be performed for itself, without being called from process 1 or process 2. Thus, it is different from a sub-process which depends on the parent process. A normal sub-process cannot be called from a different process. The re-use of processes is only possible with independent processes which are included via call activities.

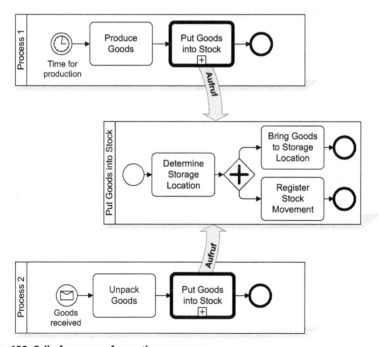

Figure 120: Call of a process from other processes

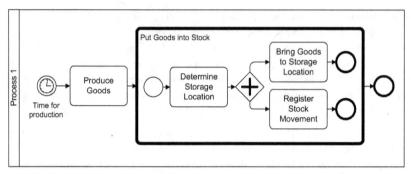

Figure 121: Expanded view of a called process

An expanded presentation as in figure 121 is also possible. Although it graphically appears as if "Put Goods into Stock" were a part of Process 1, this process is still defined independently. An expanded presentation of Process 2 would display the same details within the expanded call activity symbol. Modeling tools have the problem that changes in a called process need to be reflected in all process diagrams with an expanded call activity referring to that process. Therefore, the collapsed presentation from figure 120 would be more practical in most situations.

Since a called process is an independent process, it can also contain lanes. The activities can be located in other lanes than the call activity in the calling process. This means that the lane will be changed when the called process is started, and thus e.g. the performing role. In this case, the lane containing the call activity only indicates who is responsible for calling the other process and for handing over the required information. Of course, a called process can also contain message flows to other pools.

A normal sub-process should only have one start event, which should be untyped (cf. chapter 7.1). A called process, on the other hand, can have several start events. Exactly one of them should be an untyped event.

In figure 122, the process "Put Goods into Stock" has not only an untyped start event, but also a catching message start event. When this event occurs, the process is started as an independent process, i.e. without being called from another process. When called by a call activity, the process starts with the untyped start event, just like when it is triggered from the outside, e.g. by a user of a business process management system who selects and starts the process with a mouse-click.

Like a global task, the design of a process which may be called several times must be globally valid, so that this process is independent from the calling process. Here again, clear interfaces need to be defined.

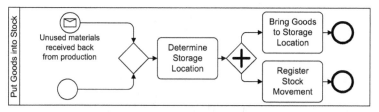

Figure 122: Called process with two start events (untyped and message)

In chapter 7.1, a sub-process "Review Application" has been discussed. It was proposed to use the attribute "result" for communicating the sub-process's result to the parent process. This attribute must be available to both the parent process and the sub-process. It is defined for the entire job application process, and it is also visible in the sub-process "Review Application", so that the sub-process can assign its result to that attribute. It is then available in the parent process.

This implies that the sub-process "Review Application" depends on the parent process. The dependency is caused by using the parent process's attribute. If this sub-process was re-used anywhere in another process, it would not work, because it would have to access the attribute "result" of the job application process.

To become re-usable, the sub-process "Review Application" must not access any attributes from the parent process. Interfaces have to be defined so that information between the parent process and the child process can still be exchanged. It must be specified which values are passed to the re-usable sub-process, and which values are returned.

Programmers know this principle: Called functions or methods should not access global variables because this would cause a narrow dependency. Independent functions or methods receive the required values as parameters, returning the results afterward.

Such interfaces are usually not graphically modeled. The exact way of specifying interfaces also depends on the tool used. A possibility for visualizing input and output data will be described in chapter 10 in the context of data objects.

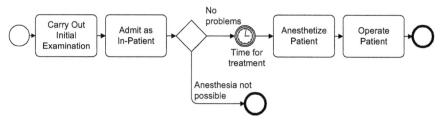

Figure 123: Example process of a treatment in a hospital

The described distinction between sub-processes and called processes is not only relevant for executable processes. It can also be found on a business level. If a sub-process, for example, is always carried out by the same people and only in one parent process, then the communication between these two processes will not be very difficult. Sometimes, however, a part of a process will be outsourced to a service provider or a shared service center. They may carry out the same partial process as a service for different other processes. In such a case, the interface must also be defined, i.e. which information items, documents, etc. have to be exchanged.

7.6 Examples of Sub-Processes and Called Processes

A process is a genuine sub-process if it depends on the parent process. It may access data from the parent process as described above, or it may depend on previous activities or decisions of the parent process. A sub-process is used for enclosing and hiding details, thus making the parent process model more concise. The contents of the sub-process nevertheless remain an inseparable part of the parent process, and they do not make any sense without the parent process.

The process for a treatment in hospital provides an example (figure 123). First, an initial examination is carried out, followed by the admission as an in-patient. If the initial examination has confirmed that there are no problems concerning an anesthesia, the process waits for the time for treatment. At this point, the patient is anesthetized and then operated. Of course, this process does not represent the real process in a hospital, in which different kinds of treatments are carried out (some with anesthesia, some without), as well as further examinations, etc. The model is only an example for illustrating sub-processes and called processes.

It may be decided to combine the activities "Anesthetize Patient" and "Operate Patient" into a sub-process. The reason is that anesthetization and operation are detailed activities that are closely related. In larger models, the creation of sub-processes would also help to reduce the complexity of the top-level model.

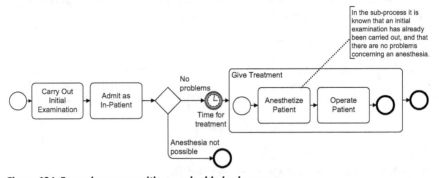

Figure 124: Example process with an embedded sub-process

96

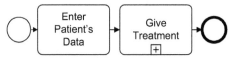

Figure 125: Incorrect re-use of the sub-process within an ambulatory treatment

A close look at the new sub-process "Give Treatment" in figure 124 reveals that this sub-process must not be isolated from the context of the main process. Before the patient can be anesthetized, it must be confirmed that there are no medical objections. In the main process, this has been confirmed by the initial examination (although this may be different in real hospitals). The sub-process "knows" that potential problems concerning anesthesia have already been ruled out. Therefore, it is possible to anesthetize the patient without any further examination.

If it were possible to re-use this sub-process in another process, it could be included into a process of an ambulatory treatment as in figure 125. The resulting overall process is incorrect and even dangerous; because even those patients would be anesthetized whose state of health does not allow this. The consequences would be fatal. Strictly speaking, the sub-process is not reused. It is rather a copy which is no longer connected to the sub-process from figure 124. It can be modified independently from the original sub-process.

The described sub-process is not re-usable because it depends on the parent process, as described above. A re-usable, callable process must be independent from the calling process. Interfaces must be defined for exchanging data.

Figure 126 shows a re-usable process for giving a treatment. The calling process needs to provide the information whether an examination has already been made. If so, the examination results are also provided.

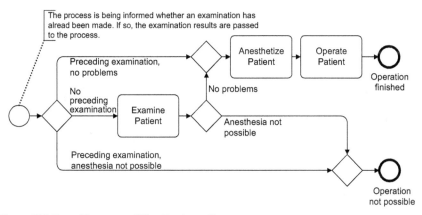

Figure 126: Reusable process "Give Treatment"

97

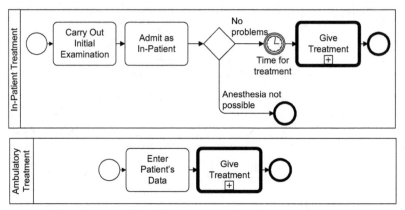

Figure 127: Calling the process from figure 126

Based on the provided information, a missing examination is performed, and it is decided whether an anesthesia is possible. This process can be reused without any problems. There is a specified interface, there are no further preconditions for the calling process, and the called process does not access data of the calling process – except those data that are passed explicitly. Therefore, the process can be used for both the in-patient treatment and the ambulatory treatment, without any modifications (figure 127).

8 Handling Exceptions

8.1 Interrupting Intermediate Events

Usually, it is rather easy to model the normal process flow. Capturing and document-
ting special cases and exceptions is more complicated and laborious. BPMN contains
several specific constructs for modeling and handling exceptions.

When an activity is carried out, sometimes an event occurs that results in an early
abortion of that activity. When writing an examination, it may happen that the time is
over before the candidate has finished. Thus, the timer event "Time over" occurs during "Writing Examination". This causes the activity to be aborted.

This is modeled by attaching an interrupting event to an activity, i.e. by placing it on
the border's activity (figure 128). Since the event occurs while the process is being carried out, it is an intermediate event. The activity "Write Examination" now has two
outgoing sequence flows: a normal one, originating directly from the activity, and an
exception flow that starts at the attached intermediate event.

If the event "Time over" does not occur during the examination, the activity will be finished regularly. A token is passed via the normal sequence flow to the activity "Submit Examination Sheet".

However, if the event does occur, the activity will be aborted, and a token will be
released via the downwards outgoing exception flow. The next activity is then "Collect
Examination Sheet" (carried out by the examination supervisor). No token will be
passed anymore to "Submit Examination Sheet" since the activity has been aborted.
The attached event only has an effect if it occurs while the activity is being performed.
If it occurs earlier or later, it will be ignored.

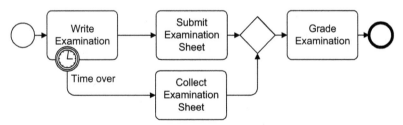

Figure 128: Abortion of an activity by a timer intermediate event

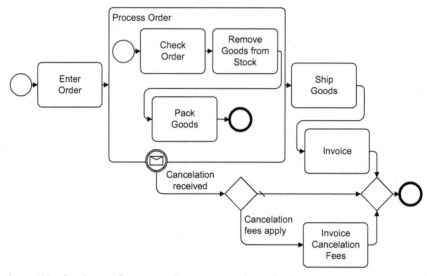

Figure 129: Aborting a sub-process when a message is received

An interrupting event can also be attached to a sub-process. In the process shown in figure 129, the entire sub-process "Process Order" is aborted when a cancelation is received. In this case, everything that happens within the process is completely terminated. If one of the three activities is being executed at that moment, it will be aborted. Activities that have not been started yet will not be executed anymore. When the sub-process is aborted, all tokens will be removed from within that sub-process, and a token will be emitted via the exception flow at the interrupting event.

If the order has been completely processed, in this example no cancelations are possible anymore. If a cancelation arrives nevertheless, it will be ignored.

When an attached intermediate event is used, it is also possible to leave the activity only through that event.

In figure 130, the daily work of a security guard has been modeled. Since there is no natural ending for the activity "Guard Building", it is always finished by the timer

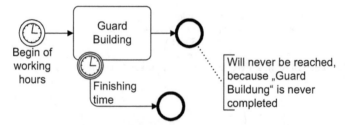

Figure 130: The activity will always be left via the interrupting event

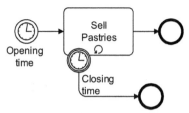

Figure 131: A loop activity that is aborted by an attached intermediate event

event "Finishing time". Here, the regular end event is not useful since it will never be reached. However, BPMN requires it. If there are any start events in a model, then every activity needs to have a regular outgoing sequence flow.

The model in figure 131 is not so ideal. The activity "Sell Pastries" will be repeated until the closing time is reached. The problem is that the activity is aborted at once when the timer event occurs. If the salesperson is just in the middle of selling some pastries, in real life, he or she will complete the sale before finishing the work.

This example can be modeled in a better way according to figure 132. Here a loop with a terminating condition is used. This condition is evaluated only when each loop repetition has been finished. Therefore, a selling activity at closing time will be completed before the process is finished.

8.2 Non-Interrupting Intermediate Events

There is another variant of the attached intermediate event. In the previous models, the occurrence of the event always resulted in an abortion of the activity. Sometimes, however, it is desired to react to such an event, but still to continue the ongoing activity. In figure 133, the customer should be notified if his order has not been completed within five days, but the processing of the order must not be interrupted.

This can be indicated by using a dashed line for the intermediate event's double border. If the event "5 days after order processing has begun" is reached before the activity has been finished, a newly created token will be passed via the exception flow to the task "Notify about Intermediate Status". After this task, the token flows to the lower end event where it will be swallowed.

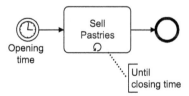

Figure 132: Improved process

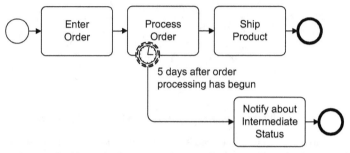

Figure 133: The attached intermediate event does not interrupt the activity

At the same time, the original token still remains in the activity "Process Order". When this task is finished, the original token is moved via the regular sequence flow, and the product is shipped. The process is finished when both tokens have reached their end events.

An attached non-interrupting event simply creates an additional token if it occurs during the execution of the respective activity. If both sequence flows should be merged by a gateway, it is not possible to use an exclusive gateway, since more than one token may arrive. A parallel gateway neither would be correct since only sometimes there will be a token in the lower sequence flow. Thus, an inclusive gateway would be required.

The message event also has a non-interrupting variant. In figure 134 the reception of an inquiry concerning an order triggers the task "Answer Inquiry". The order is further processed in parallel.

Besides timer and message events, the following types of intermediate events (described in chapter 6.4) can be attached to activities: Signal events, conditional events, multiple events, and parallel multiple events (figure 135). Each of them can be used as an interrupting or a non-interrupting event, the latter with a dashed border. Of course, non-interrupting intermediate events not only can be attached to tasks, but also to sub-processes.

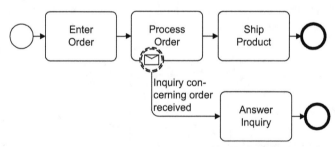

Figure 134: The non-interrupting version of the attached message event

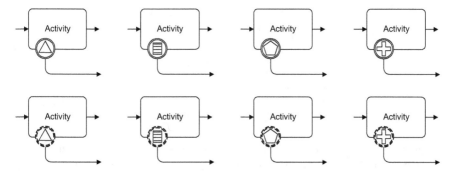

Figure 135: Types of attached intermediate events: Signal, condition, multiple, parallel multiple. At the top the interrupting versions; at the bottom the non-interrupting versions.

8.3 Handling of Errors

The handling of exceptions is quite often required because of an error. For this, intermediate events of type "error" can be used. They are marked with a flash symbol. In contrast to the previous types of intermediate events, error intermediate events cannot be used within normal sequence flows. They can only be attached to activity boundaries.

Figure 136 contains a process in a laboratory. First an analysis is conducted, and then the results are evaluated. Should the analysis reveal that the equipment is defective, this would be an error which prevents the normal execution of the process. For this case, there is an exception flow in which the sample is sent to an external laboratory.

The activity to be aborted by an error event may also be a sub-process. In this subprocess, it is possible to model kind and origin of the respective error. Therefore, the catching error event is complemented with its throwing counterpart.

Figure 137 shows a sub-process with two throwing error events. After taking a sample, the sub-process is started. First the sample is analyzed. This is usually followed by checking the result. If the result is plausible, the sub-process finishes. If the result is not

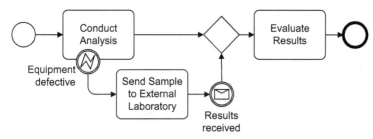

Figure 136: When an error occurs, an exception flow is started

103

plausible, this is an error, and the throwing error end event "Result not plausible" is reached. In this case, the sub-process is aborted, and the thrown error is caught by the error intermediate event at the sub-process boundary. In this case, the exception flow is followed, and the activity "Arrange for External Analysis" is triggered.

In the sub-process, another error may occur: If during the activity "Analyze Sample" it turns out that the equipment is defective (here also modeled with a catching error event), it will be repaired. If the repair has been successful, the analysis of the sample will be started again. In the case of an unsuccessful repair, the throwing error event "Equipment out of order" occurs. Again, the sub-process is aborted, and the error is thrown to the intermediate error event that triggers the exception flow to the activity "Arrange for External Analysis".

Like in the other event types, the filled icon stands for a throwing event, while a catching event is represented by a blank icon. Throwing error events are always end events, because they completely abort the surrounding sub-process. Catching error events, on the other hand, are always intermediate events. They can only be attached to the boundaries of tasks or sub-processes.

In figure 137 there are two different throwing error events in the sub-process. Since the error intermediate event at the boundary does not have a label, it catches any kind of error from the sub-process – regardless from which error event it is thrown.

In some cases, however, it may be necessary to have different exception flows for different errors. For this, several catching error events can be attached to the sub-process boundary. If they are labeled with the names of the throwing error events, each event will only react to errors thrown by an error event of the same name.

The model in figure 138 makes use of this. If the error "Result not plausible" occurs, an external analysis should be arranged, as in the previous model. If the error "Equipment out of order" occurs instead, repair by the manufacturer should be arranged in addition to the external analysis.

If there are several error intermediate events attached to a sub-process boundary, they should always be labeled. Since an unlabeled error intermediate event always catches any type of error, it also reacts to errors with own labeled events. The implicit parallel flows resulting from such a combination of labeled and unlabeled events would be difficult to understand.

8.4   Escalation Events

Escalation events are similar to error events. While error events are mainly used for technical problems, escalation events primarily stand for problems on a business level, e.g. if a task is not completed, a goal is not reached, or a required agreement is not achieved.

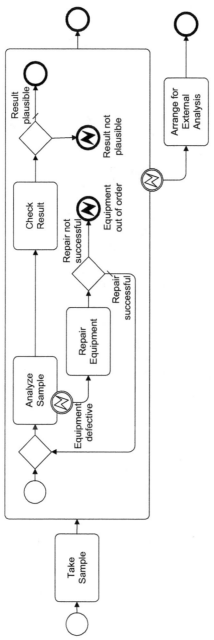

Figure 137: Errors occurring in the sub-process are forwarded to the error intermediate event at the boundary

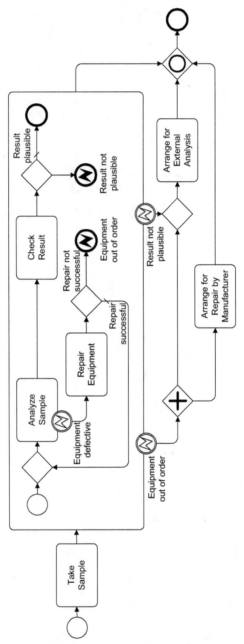

Figure 138: Different exception flows are triggered by named error events

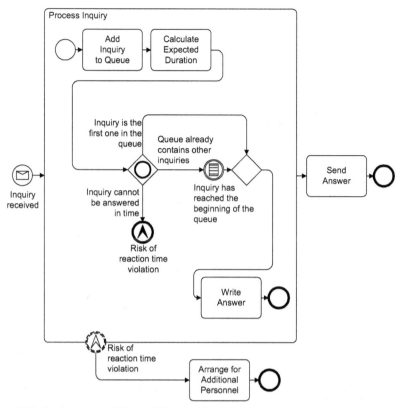

Figure 139: A sub-process with escalation events

Like throwing error events, throwing escalation events can be used in sub-processes. An escalation is caught by an escalation intermediate event with the same name, attached to the sub-process border. The intermediate event again triggers an exception flow.

In contrast to errors which always abort the activity, escalations come in both variants: The interrupting and the non-interrupting event. Non-interrupting escalation events are regarded as the default.

The example of figure 139 starts with adding an incoming inquiry to a queue. After that, the expected duration for answering the inquiry is calculated. This expected duration depends on the length of the queue. If it turns out that the inquiry cannot be answered within the promised reaction time, a token flows to the throwing escalation end event. The escalation is caught by the non-interrupting escalation intermediate event at the sub-process's boundary. This event then emits a token and triggers the activity "Arrange for Additional Personnel".

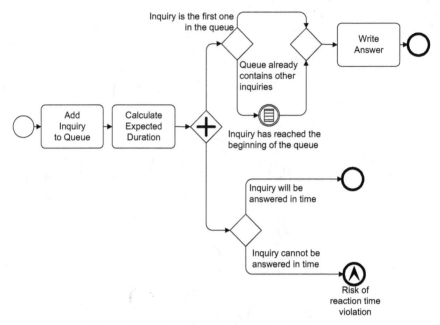

Figure 140: Alternative model of the sub-process from figure 139

Since it is a non-interrupting intermediate event, the sub-process continues in parallel. If the inquiry is the first one in the queue, an answer will be written without delay. Otherwise, if the queue already contains other inquiries, it must be waited until all of them are completed. This is indicated by the conditional event "Inquiry has reached the beginning of the queue". When this event has occurred, the answer is written and finally sent to the customer in the main process.

It may be confusing that there is an exclusive gateway for merging the two sequence flows because they originate from an inclusive gateway. However, if the conditions at the inclusive gateway are analyzed, it turns out that in any case exactly one of these conditions becomes true. Therefore, the merging by an exclusive gateway is correct. As an alternative, the model of the sub-process could be a bit more extensive, as in figure 140, which on the other hand requires more space.

Since an escalation usually does not abort the sub-process, it is not only possible to use an end event for throwing an escalation, but also an intermediate event (figure 141).

If an escalation is required to abort the entire activity, the attached intermediate event's boundaries are drawn with solid lines (figure 142). In such a case, the throwing escalation event in the sub-process must be an end event. If a throwing escalation intermediate event were used, the subsequent sequence flow could never occur because the sub-process would be aborted by the escalation.

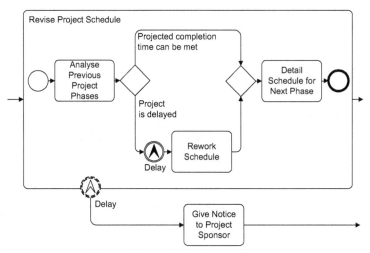

Figure 141: Sub-process with throwing escalation intermediate event

As in the case of error intermediate events, there can be several escalation intermediate events which can be distinguished by their names.

8.5 Event Sub-Processes

In contrast to an ordinary sub-process, an event sub-process is not triggered by a sequence flow, but by an event occurring during process execution. Therefore, an event sub-process does neither have any incoming nor any outgoing sequence flows.

Figure 143 shows a simplified software development process. At the beginning the requirements are determined, followed by the development. It may involve several iterations. Each iteration is planned before the planned features are implemented. The iteration steps are repeated until the software is completed.

In most software projects, change requests arise during the development. These are handled in the event sub-process "Process Change Request". The dotted boundary distinguishes the event sub-process from a normal sub-process. It is triggered by the event "Change request received" – but only if this occurs while the main process is

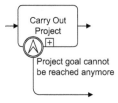

Figure 142: Interrupting escalation intermediate event

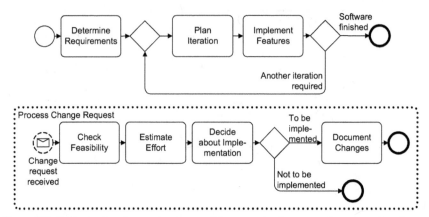

Figure 143: Software development process with an event sub-process for processing change requests

running. The start event's border is dashed, i.e. it is a non-interrupting start event. The main process is therefore continued while the event sub-process is carried out. In this special sub-process first the feasibility of the required change is checked, and then the effort is estimated, and a decision is made about the implementation. If the change is to be implemented, it will be documented. In the main process, this documented change will be implemented in one of the following iterations.

During software development, several change requests may arise. Accordingly, the event sub-process can be performed several times. Several simultaneous instances of the event sub-process are also possible.

There is also the possibility to abort the surrounding process when an event sub-process is started. In this case, the start event is drawn with the normal solid line.

Figure 144 shows the sub-process "Produce Chemicals". This sub-process itself contains two event sub-processes. The first one, "Adjust System", is non-interrupting, as can be seen by the dashed line of the conditional start event. The system may be adjusted several times during production. By contrast, an error of the type "Critical problem" not only starts the second event sub-process "Conduct Emergency Shut-Off", but it also aborts the process "Produce Chemicals". This is indicated by the fact that start event's border is not dashed, but solid.

The interrupting event sub-process "Conduct Emergency Shut-Off" can be started only once during the execution of the sub-process "Produce Chemicals", because after all this process is aborted. If the event sub-process ended in a normal untyped end event, a token would be emitted to the surrounding process's outgoing sequence flow. In this example, however, an error end event is used, which again throws an error. This error is caught by the attached error intermediate event "Emergency shut-off", and a token is emitted to the exception flow.

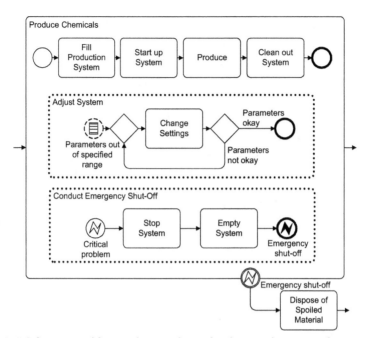

Figure 144: Sub-process with a non-interrupting and an interrupting event sub-process

A start event of type "error" can only be used in event sub-processes. There is no dashed variant of the error start event, i.e. such an event can only trigger interrupting event sub-processes.

Most other event types can be used both as interrupting and non-interrupting events. Besides message events and conditional events, this is also true for timer events, signal events, multiple events, and parallel multiple events. In contrast to normal processes, the escalation event here can also be used as a starting event. The non-interrupting variants of the aforementioned events are only allowed within an event sub-process, but not in a normal process. Untyped start events, on the other hand, cannot be used in event sub-processes.

In the next chapter, the compensation event will be introduced as a further event type that can also be used as a start event in an event sub-process, but only as an interrupting event.

As it is known from normal sub-processes, event sub-processes can also be drawn in a collapsed state (figure 145). Like the expanded versions they have dotted boundary lines. In addition to this, the respective start event of each process is shown in the upper left corner. This event's boundary – solid or dashed – shows whether the surrounding process is aborted or not.

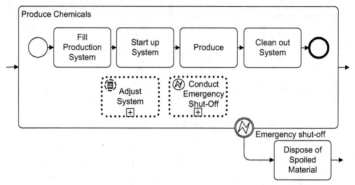

Figure 145: Collapsed event sub-processes

9 Transactions and Compensations

9.1 Modeling of Transactions

The term "transaction" is used in different contexts. For example, there are business transactions, such as a money transfer from one bank account to another. In computer science, especially database transactions are well-known. The different types of transactions have in common that they are always complete units of work. A transaction can either be carried out in its entirety, or not at all. If something goes wrong, the transaction must be rolled back.

During a money transfer, it might turn out that the receiver's account number does not exist. Then the money must be transferred back. If the computer crashes while a customer data set is being saved, the database system will roll back the database to the original state before the saving operation had been started. Thus, it prevents incomplete data sets causing an inconsistent state of the database.

Parts of business processes can also be treated as transactions. A typical example is the booking of a journey which involves separate bookings of a flight and a hotel. The booking of the entire journey is only successful if both the flight and the hotel have been booked successfully. If the hotel has been booked and it then turns out that there is no flight available anymore, the booking of the journey has not been entirely completed. In this case, the hotel booking needs to be reversed, i.e. it must be canceled at the hotel. Since such booking procedures including inquiries and answers may take many days, business process transactions are also called long-running transactions.

For modeling transactions, the process from figure 129 in chapter 8.1 is used again. There, the sub-process "Process Order" will be aborted when the event "Cancelation received" occurs. According to the model, a cancelation fee may be invoiced. Apart from that, the process is finished.

A closer look reveals that in fact the abortion of a sub-process entails further activities. In the sub-process, first the order is checked, then the goods are removed from stock, and finally they are packed. Depending on the point in time the cancelation arrives, it is possible that the goods have already been removed from stock or packed. In these cases, it is necessary to put the goods back into stock, or first to unpack and then put them back into stock.

Thus, the effects of the activities already completed must be reversed. This can be reached by defining compensating activities for the sub-process's activities. "Check Order" does not need to be compensated. The compensating activity for "Remove Goods from Stock" is "Put Goods into Stock". "Pack Goods" is compensated by "Unpack Goods".

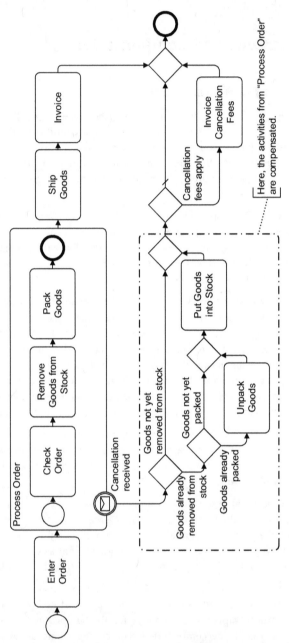

Figure 146: When a cancelation message is received, the effects of the finished activities are reversed

Figure 146 shows how the required compensations could be modeled with basic BPMN constructs. When the interrupting event occurs, it needs to be distinguished whether the goods have already been removed from stock. If this is not the case, nothing needs to be done.

If the goods have already been removed from stock, it must be determined whether they are already packed. In this case, the activity "Unpack Goods" will be carried out first. In both cases, the goods will then be put into stock again.

The rounded rectangle with the dash-dotted line is a group. It only serves presentation purposes, such as highlighting interesting parts of a model, or grouping elements that belong together, as it is the case here. The control flow logic of the model is not influenced by a group (cf. chapter 13.1)

This model is rather intricate. The handling of the exception is larger than the normal flow. It can be easily imagined what would happen if a sub-process contained many more activities which could be executed in various sequences. The part of the model containing the compensations would become very huge since all possible combinations of completed activities would need to be distinguished.

Another way of modeling this case is shown in figure 147. Here the border of the sub-process "Process Order" is drawn with a double line, thus marking the sub-process as a transaction. A transaction must either be carried out completely or not at all. This means that aborting a transaction automatically reverses the effects of the activities that have already been executed. In order to enable this, a compensation activity is assigned to each activity that requires compensation.

The activity "Put Goods into Stock", for example, contains a rewind symbol (two arrowheads), identifying it as a compensation activity. It compensates the activity "Remove Goods from Stock". This assignment is modeled with a compensation association and a compensation intermediate event attached to the boundary of the activity to be compensated. Not only tasks but also sub-processes can be marked with a rewind-symbol and be used as compensating activities.

Catching intermediate events of the compensation type are only used for this purpose. They are always attached to an activity, and they always have outgoing compensation associations running to the compensating activity. The compensation association is a dotted line with an arrow. It must not be confused with message flow.

The activity "Check Order" does not have a compensating activity, because it does not have any effects that need to be reversed. It would not make sense to "uncheck" a checked order.

If the transaction is aborted, it will be checked which activities have already been carried out. Only for these activities, the assigned compensation activities will be executed one after another – in the reversed order of the original activities.

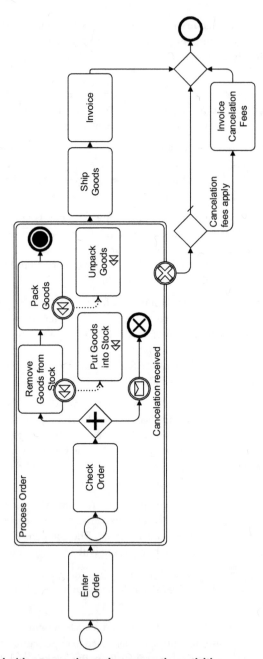

Figure 147: Model with a transaction and compensating activities

What does this mean for the example process? If only the activity "Check Order" has been carried out, no compensation takes place in case of cancelation, because there is no compensation defined for this activity. If the goods have already been removed from stock, they will be put back into stock. If the goods are even packed, they will first be unpacked and then put into stock again. Thus, the flow following an abortion of the sub-process "Process Order" is exactly the same as the exception flow in figure 146 involving several gateways.

How is a transaction aborted? One possibility is to trigger the abortion from the outside. If the process is executed by a process engine, an administrator can react to an error that cannot be handled otherwise by aborting the process via the engine's administration component.

In such a case, first the compensation activities are carried out, as described above. Then a token is passed to the modeled exception flow. For this, there is a catching intermediate event attached to the transaction boundary. This intermediate event type is called "cancel" and contains a blank cross. The cancel intermediate event indicates that the sub-process is not just aborted, but the compensations will be carried out first.

In the case of serious errors, it may happen that it is not possible anymore to abort the transaction normally, including compensations. A defect in the storage equipment may cause not only the need to abort the transaction, but it may also inhibit putting goods into storage. For such a case it is possible to add another exception flow without previous compensations. This could be modeled with a normal error intermediate event attached to the transaction boundary. However, in practice, it is not feasible to model every conceivable case.

The normal abortion of a transaction can not only be triggered from the outside, but also from within the process. This is modeled by an end event of type "cancel". Its symbol is a filled diagonal cross. If this end event is reached, the entire process will be aborted, just as when a terminate end event is reached. In the case of the cancel end event, however, the required compensations are carried out, and then the exception flow starts at the catching cancel intermediate event.

In the example, the transaction must be aborted when the event "Cancelation received" occurs. While in the model of figure 146 the catching message intermediate event is attached to the sub-process boundary, this is not possible for a transaction. A normal interrupting intermediate event would trigger the exception flow without performing the compensations, as described above.

A catching cancel intermediate event must be used instead. This is triggered when a throwing cancel end event is reached within the transaction. Therefore, two parallel paths are created by the parallel gateway. In the sequence flow at the top, the activities are performed. At the same time, the parallel sequence flow at the bottom waits for the occurrence of the intermediate event "Cancelation received". If this intermediate event occurs, the cancel end event is reached, i.e. the transaction is aborted. Then the required compensations are carried out and the exception flow at the attached cancel intermediate event is triggered. Since the cancel event aborts the entire transaction, the path at the top is aborted, as well.

If the transaction is not aborted, the end event of the upper path finally will be reached. In this case the bottom path is still active, i.e. a token still waits for the reception of a cancelation. Therefore, it would not be correct to use an untyped end event because this would only terminate the upper path. Instead, a terminate end event is used that finishes the entire transaction sub-process, including the lower path. In this case, the transaction has been completed successfully, and the process continues with the normal sequence flow. The next activity to be performed is "Ship Goods".

9.2 Direct Call of Compensations

Compensations can be modeled without transactions, as well. For this, throwing compensation end or intermediate events can be used. They contain filled rewind-symbols.

In figure 148, the process for booking and approving a business trip has been modeled. Here it is assumed that the travel will only be approved when the exact dates and prices of hotel and transport have been provided. Therefore, in this process, the booking activities take place before approval.

The activities "Book Flight" and "Book Hotel" both have compensation activities assigned. However, these activities are not part of a transaction, so that the compensations cannot be triggered by aborting a transaction. They must be called explicitly.

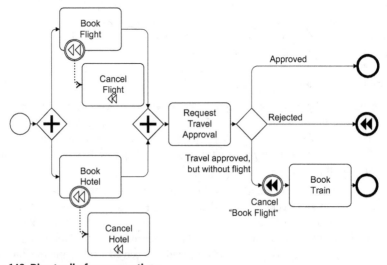

Figure 148: Direct call of compensations

118

The exclusive gateway after requesting the approval has three exits. In the first case, the request is approved, and the process finishes with an untyped end event. There are no compensations required. In the second case, the request is completely rejected. The sequence flow runs to a throwing compensation end event. This event does not have any label. Thus, it triggers the compensation of all completed activities in reverse order. Both the flight and the hotel booking are canceled. The activity "Request Travel Approval" does not have a compensation activity, so it is not compensated.

In the third case, the travel is approved, but it is not approved to travel by plane. Therefore, only the activity "Book Flight" must be compensated, but not the activity "Book Hotel". This is indicated by naming the activity to be canceled in the label of the throwing intermediate compensation event. If required, it is also possible to specify several activities in the label of a throwing compensation event. In this example, however, only the compensation activity "Cancel Flight" is carried out. Afterwards, a train journey is booked, and the process is finished.

In this model, it is not possible to book a train in the first place. This, of course, is not very reasonable, but the model should be kept rather compact in order to illustrate the essence of the BPMN structure to be illustrated, just like all examples in this intro-ductory book.

9.3 Event Sub-Processes for Compensations

Compensations can also be handled by event sub-processes. They have compensation start events. In contrast, to other event sub-processes as discussed in chapter 8.5, they are not triggered by an event of the surrounding process. Instead, they are started when a throwing compensation event of the same name occurs after that process. Thus, the event sub-process will only be performed after the surrounding process has been finished.

The border of the compensation start event is always drawn as a solid line. In normal event sub-processes, this indicates that the surrounding process is aborted. Since a cancelation is only carried out when the surrounding sub-process is already finished, there is no distinction between a non-interrupting and an interrupting compensation start event.

In figure 149, a travel agency organizes the visit of a festival for its customers. For this, they first book the journey and then the tickets for the festival. The activity "Book Journey" has a compensation activity; the festival tickets, on the other hand, cannot be returned.

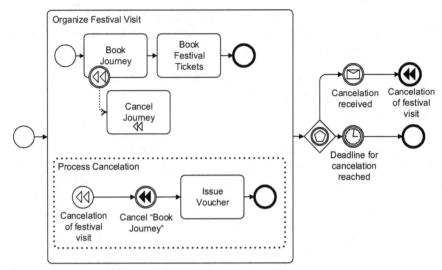

Figure 149: Event sub-process with compensation start event

After the festival visit has been organized, the process waits until either the deadline is over, or a cancelation is received from the customer. In this case, the compensation end event "Cancelation of festival visit" is reached. Now the event sub-process is started via the compensation start event with the same name as the throwing end event. In the event sub-process, the compensation for "Book Journey" is triggered. Since unfortunately the festival ticket cannot be returned, the travel agency issues a voucher of a smaller amount of money to the customer which can be used when booking the next journey.

Since in the main process the end event has already been reached, the entire process is completed with the end of the "Process Cancelation" event sub-process. It would also have been possible to trigger this sub-process by a throwing compensation intermediate event, after which the process would be continued.

Such a compensating event sub-process can be used if not only the compensation activities need to be performed in the case of a cancelation, but also other activities. Although it is a bit more complicated to figure out in which case which activities have to be compensated in which order, such an event sub-process provides a sophisticated way of modeling such complex scenarios.

9.4   Use of Exceptions, Transactions, and Compensations

The concepts for modeling exceptions, transactions, and compensations, as they have been described in this and the previous chapter, originally have been developed in software technology. They are especially interesting for modeling executable workflows. In principle it is also possible to use them in business-oriented models, since errors, exceptions, cancelations, etc. also occur in non-automated processes. The examples used for the explanations have been deliberately taken from the business domain.

Some BPMN experts point out that many process models almost exclusively consider normal processes in which everything runs as expected. However, a large portion of problems and the effort involved in managing business processes results from errors, exceptions, and special cases. Therefore, they recommend to model exception flows, as well, using the special constructs provided by BPMN (cf. e.g. [Silver 2012]).

On the other hand, in contrast to the basic BPMN elements, these constructs need a lot of explanation, and they are not easy to apply. Exact models of all exceptional cases will become very large and detailed. It needs to be decided whether they yield an appropriate benefit to the target audience and whether the required effort is justified. This depends on the modeling purpose.

In principle, some of the more technical concepts can be transferred to the business level, but this may cause additional problems and questions.

For example, compensating a booking transaction in a computer system can be achieved rather easily by creating a compensating entry into the system. The above example concerning the booking of a flight or a hotel is not that easy in practice. For example, a cancelation may be ruled out for budget tickets, or it may be possible only within a certain time span, or it may cost an additional fee. In some cases, it is better to alter the person or the date of a booking instead of canceling it entirely. Each of these cases can have different effects on a process. Just modeling a compensation activity does not accurately reflect all these cases.

It needs to be decided in advance whether, how, and how detailed such cases should be modeled. This should be documented as modeling conventions.

10 Data Objects in Processes

10.1 Modeling Data Flow

When a process is carried out, it uses and creates data, information, files, documents, etc. A sequence flow from one activity to another is often accompanied by data transfer. The main purpose of message flow is also the exchange of data.

So far, when modeling sequence or message flows, data have not been considered explicitly. A sequence flow purely triggers the following activity. In respect to message flow, it is only important that a certain message is received, and thus, the related event occurs. If it is required to know which particular data are exchanged, this must be modeled separately.

BPMN was initially developed as a graphical notation for executable processes. Therefore, it was implied that all activities within a process can access all data within a pool at any time. If this concept is actually applied (e.g. by a process engine), it is not necessary to model the movement of data within a process.

However, in many processes, there is no common data pool so that it does make sense to model the data transfer explicitly. And even if there is a common data pool, it may be helpful to model input and output data of the activities. In doing so, data-related dependencies can be identified. For example, when using a common data pool, it still must be ensured that a certain piece of information has already been produced before it is required.

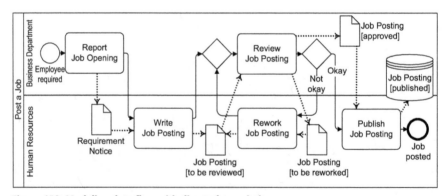

Figure 150: Modeling data flow with directed associations

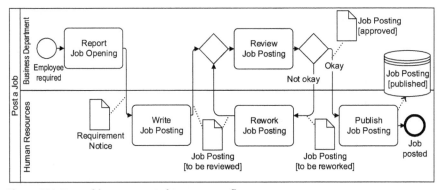

Figure 151: Data objects connected to sequence flows

Figure 150 shows how to model data flow within a process. For this purpose, data objects are used in the form of document symbols. A data object can represent any kind of data and information, such as an electronic data set, a file, or a physical document.

Directed data associations can be used for modeling data inputs and outputs of activities. The name of a data object is often appended with the object's current state, printed in square brackets. In the process in figure 150, the data object "Job Posting" can change its state from "to be reviewed" to "to be reworked" and "approved".

A data association is drawn as a dotted line. It must not be confused with the dashed message flow connectors.

Data objects only exist within a process. In order to model persistent data, a data store can be used. In figure 150, the published job posting is transferred to such a data store at the very end. Thus, it will be still available when the process has finished.

Most of the data flows shown in figure 150 run in parallel to sequence flows. In such cases, it is also possible to simply connect the data object with the sequence flow, using an undirected association (figure 151). In this example, both models are equivalent. However, it is also possible to create a data object at a certain point and to use it much later in the process. This means that the data object is not passed with the sequence flow to the directly following activity. Such a case can only be modeled with directed associations, as in figure 152.

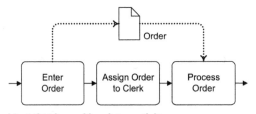

Figure 152: A data object that is used in a later activity

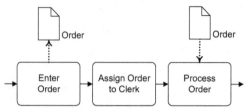

Figure 153: Alternative modeling of figure 152

A diagram can become confusing if there are too many lengthy data associations running through the entire process. It is therefore allowed to draw the same data object several times, as in figure 153. The two data object symbols do not represent two different data objects which happen to have the same name, but both actually reference the same object.

10.2 Multiple Data Objects

Often it is not only necessary to model single data sets, but also collections or lists. Such multiple data objects can be marked with three lines, just like multi-instance activities and multi-instance participants. In the first step of the process fragment in figure 154, the collection of received applications is reviewed. In doing so, the interesting applications are selected. These interesting applications are also a collection. In the second step, one single application is selected. As a single object, it naturally does not have a multiple-marker anymore.

10.3 Data and Events

Data objects only exist within a process; therefore data associations cannot cross the borders of pools. Direct data exchange with other processes is modeled with message flows (see chapter 5). In order to specify that the content of a message is processed as a data object, a catching message event can have an outgoing data association. Conversely, a throwing message event can have an incoming data association. The sent message then contains the contents of that data object (figure 155).

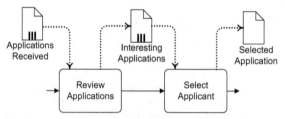

Figure 154: Multiple data objects representing lists or collections

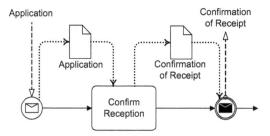

Figure 155: Events can convert messages into data objects and vice versa

10.4 Data Stores

An indirect data exchange can also be realized by one process writing into a data store, and another process reading the data from that store. This requires that both processes can access the same data store. This is often the case if both processes belong to the same organization. In figure 156, a bill of material is created within the engineering process and written into a data store. In production planning, the bill of materials is read from the data store in order to determine the materials required.

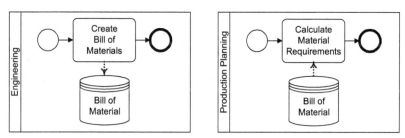

Figure 156: Two processes accessing the same data store

10.5 Passing Data to Called Activities

If a process calls another independent process via a call activity (cf. chapter 7.5), the passing of data can also be modeled with data objects.

A data association leading into a call activity means that the data object is passed to that activity. Conversely, an outgoing data association stands for the return of a called activity's data object to the calling process. However, it is not possible to pass any arbitrary data objects, because the process or global task to be called is defined elsewhere. This includes the definition of required data, as well produced and returned

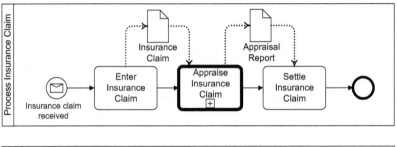

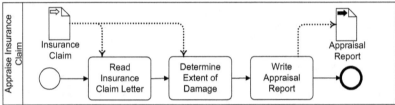

Figure 157: Modeling data input and output for called processes

data. A global task is not modeled graphically, but for a process to be called from other processes, the required input and the provided output can be modeled.

In figure 157, the process "Appraise Insurance Claim" is called from within the process "Process Insurance Claim". The process "Appraise Insurance Claim" at the bottom contains data objects with arrows representing the process's data input and data output. The arrow of a data output is filled, that of a data input is blank. A data input defines which data need to be provided to the process in order to work properly. Accordingly, a data output denotes which data are produced by the process and returned to the caller.

If a process is integrated into another process via a call activity, it must be ensured that correct data inputs are provided. Likewise, only the defined data outputs can be received back from the call activity. In the example, the insurance claim process passes an insurance claim to the called process and waits for an appraisal report which corresponds exactly to the modeled data input and output in the appraisal process. Therefore, the call will work properly.

It would be possible to model further data objects (without arrow icons) in the process "Appraise Insurance Claim". These, however, would only be used internally in the process.

If a process model contains several data inputs or outputs, the calling process must be provided with data objects suitable for all inputs, and the process will also return data objects of all data outputs. The BPMN specification also defines optional data inputs and outputs. However, this is not visible in the diagram and should be explained in an annotation, if required. Data inputs and data outputs can also be marked with three lines as multiple data objects.

10.6 Use of Data Objects

Data objects and associations, and especially the definitions of data inputs and outputs, can carry important information for process execution. For this, these elements can be connected with specific data structures, e.g. XML schema definitions. When executing a process instance, a process engine can then decide whether the required data inputs are available, and a certain activity can be triggered. Nevertheless, further detail information is required for this in addition to the model's graphical information.

On a business level, data objects provide the means to analyze and optimize processes with respect to data creation and utilization. Process models can also be connected to data models via these elements. As an example, data models, UML class diagrams, or technical terms diagrams could be used to refine data objects in process models. In doing so, the process view could be integrated with the data view. This is important for seamless information systems development. Such an integration of different views is not part of the process modeling notation. It needs to be regulated by modeling conventions and suitable modeling tools.

11 Choreographies

Chapter 5 described how collaborations are modeled using message flows between processes. In chapter 6, catching message events and event-based gateways were introduced. With these elements, it is possible to specify that a process is waiting for a message, or that a certain path is selected based on a received message.

In many cases it is required to define the co-operation of different partners. This applies e.g. for business-to-business integration. Several partners connect their information systems in such a way that placing and fulfilling orders, as well as other business transactions, can be completely automated. In such a case, every company is responsible for its own process. It is necessary, however, that all involved partners agree on the messages to be exchanged.

In order to support this, black box pools can be used, i.e. pools without their processes displayed. Figure 158 shows the collaboration for creating an advertisement. In this diagram, the message flow between customer, advertising agency, and several designers can be seen.

The approximate temporal order can be deduced from the sequence of message flows from left to right. Nevertheless, this can be ambiguous because no sequence flow is shown, and possible conditions and repetitions are not visible. In the example, an inquiry will usually be followed by an order, but not every case will involve change requests. If changes are requested, on the other hand, it is also possible to send more than one change request.

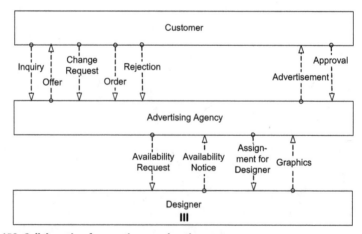

Figure 158: Collaboration for creating an advertisement

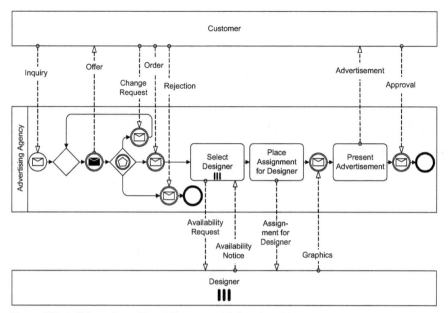

Figure 159: Collaboration with public process of the advertising agency

Presumably, only one of the two messages "Order" and "Rejection" will be sent within one process instance. Availability requests will probably be sent to several designers, but an assignment should obviously be sent to only one of these designers.

All these dependencies are not visible in the black box representation of the collaboration. One possibility for modeling the described logic is to include one or more public processes. In the example it is advantageous to model the public process of the advertising agency since all messages of the other two partners are exchanged with the advertising agency (figure 159). If there were also a direct interaction between customer and designer, at least one additional process would be necessary.

From figure 159 the exact sequence of message exchanges can be deduced. It can be seen, for example, that it is possible to send several change requests, each of which is answered by the advertising agency with a new offer. It is also visible that several availability requests are sent to designers, but only one assignment. The model does not clearly show that the assignment is sent to one selected designer (and not perhaps one single assignment to all designers). For this, it would be necessary either to model an additional pool for the selected designer or to display the designer's process, which could specify that all designers wait for the assignment for a certain time span. Only the designer who has received the assignment will send graphics. The others finish their processes.

In the presented process, many possibilities are not covered, e.g. it is assumed that the customer always reacts to an offer. Likewise, it is expected that a designer always sends graphics after having received an assignment. The case that one partner does not react within a certain period could be modeled with event-based gateways and timer events.

11.1 Choreography Diagrams

Choreography diagrams provide another possibility for modeling the temporal and logical sequence of message flows in the scenario described above. In these diagrams, the focus is on the message exchanges themselves. They are modeled as choreography activities.

Figure 160 contains the choreography for the example of creating an advertisement which has already been shown as a collaboration. A choreography activity represents the exchange of one or more messages between two or more partners. In the simplest case, it comprises sending only one message from one partner to another. An example is the choreography activity "Send Inquiry", in which a customer sends the message "Inquiry" to an advertising agency. A choreography activity can also represent several message flows. Within "Get Approval", first a message with an advertisement is sent from the advertising agency to the customer, and then the customer sends back a message with the approval.

The presented choreography is easy to understand. First, an inquiry is sent (from the customer to the advertising agency), followed by an offer (from the advertising agency to the customer). Then there are three possibilities: Firstly, it is possible to send a change request. In this case, the choreography activity "Send Offer" will be repeated.

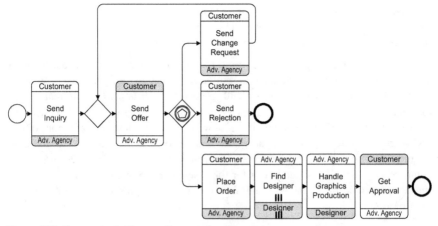

Figure 160: Choreography for creating an advertisement

Secondly, a rejection can be sent, and the choreography is finished. In the third case, an order is placed, followed by finding an appropriate designer. The activity "Find Designer" is carried out several times. Besides the advertising agency, each time one member of the group of designers is involved. Finally, the message exchanges "Handle Graphics Production" and "Get Approval" follow.

Each choreography activity is initiated from one of the partners by sending the first message. This initiating partner is shown in a white band at the upper or lower edge of the choreography activity symbol. The name of the other participant is placed in a shaded field at the other edge. The modeler can freely decide which partner is placed at the top and which at the bottom. If there are several choreography activities involving the same partners, the placement will usually be the same in all choreography activities. If an additional collaboration is modeled for the same scenario, it is adviceable to reflect the collaboration's arrangement of pools. Accordingly, the choreography activities in figure 160 have the customer at the top and the advertising agency at the bottom, respectively the advertising agency at the top and the designers at the bottom.

The choreography activity "Find Designer" contains a multiple marker, i.e. it is carried out several times. Since the involved partner also has a multiple marker, the message exchange involves one single designer in each repetition. Here, the number of repetitions is known in advance. If this is not the case, the choreography activity receives the loop marker, which is already known from normal activities (figure 161).

In this example, there are only two partners involved in each choreography activity. For more partners, additional participant bands can be placed at the edges. Thereby always only one field is colored white because only one of the partners initiates the message exchange by a first message. An example can be found in figure 165.

In a choreography diagram, a sequence flow is defined for the choreography activities. It is basically modeled like the sequence flow in normal processes.

However, some process modeling elements are not meaningful in choreography diagrams. Therefore, they are not allowed here. For example, there are no message events within normal sequence flow, because message exchanges are contained in the choreography activities by definition. Likewise, the event-based gateway in figure 160 is not followed by events, but by choreography activities. This means that the path is selected by the choreography activity which is first started by its initiating message.

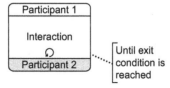

Figure 161: A looping choreography activity

131

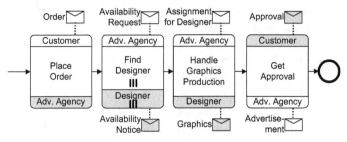

Figure 162: Choreography activities with message icons

If one wants to know which messages are exchanged in each choreography activity, small envelope symbols can be added and connected with the respective partner's band (figure 162). The envelopes have the same colors as their partner bands. A white envelope signifies a message that initiates a choreography activity. The envelope symbols of the other messages are shaded.

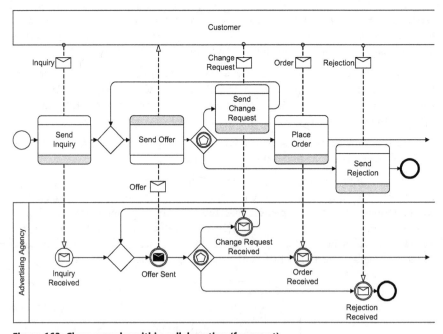

Figure 163: Choreography within collaboration (fragment)

11.2 Choreography within Collaboration

The choreography is closely related to the respective collaboration. If this relation should be shown, a choreography can be included in a collaboration diagram. Figure 163 shows a part of the advertisement process in which the choreography has been inserted into the collaboration diagram from figure 159.

Since choreographies display the sequence of message exchanges, the choreography activities are placed between the pools. The related message flows run from pool to pool, as in normal collaboration diagrams. Here they run through the respective choreography activities. Thus, choreographies and collaborations are connected via the message flows.

The related partners, therefore, can be identified by the sources and the targets of the message flows, so the names of the partners need not to be shown in the choreography activities. They still contain the participants' bands in order to remain clearly identifiable as choreography activities and to be distinguished from normal activities. Again, the initiating messages are blank; the others are shaded (figure 164).

It can be helpful to include a choreography into a collaboration to validate that the logic of the message exchange within the own process is in accordance with the choreography.

11.3 Choreography Sub-Processes

Like normal activities, choreography activities can be organized hierarchically. Besides choreography tasks which cannot be decomposed further, there are choreography sub-

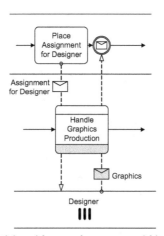

Figure 164: Choreography activity with several messages, within a collaboration (fragment)

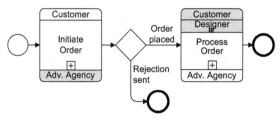

Figure 165: Choreography with collapsed sub-processes

processes which comprise more detailed choreographies. They are marked with a small '+'. In figure 165, the above choreography has been re-arranged into two sub-processes. They are shown in the collapsed state, i.e. the internal details of the sub-processes are not visible.

"Process Order" is an example that illustrates how to draw a choreography activity with more than two participants. There is always only one white participant's band, because only one participant initiates the choreography activity. Multiple participants' bands are distributed in such a way that the difference of the numbers of bands at the

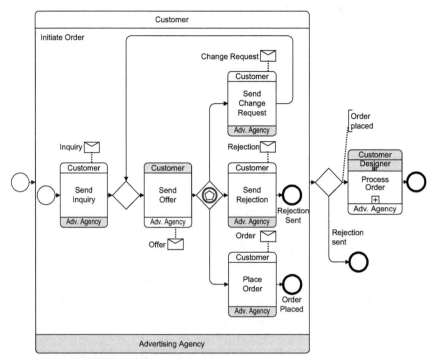

Figure 166: Expanded choreography sub-process

top and of those at the bottom is not more than one. An initiating participant, with a white band, can also be placed together with one or more other participants with shaded bands, at the same edge.

For each sub-process, there is a detailed choreography which can either be modeled in a separate choreography diagram, or inserted into the expanded sub-process symbol, as in figure 166. In order to make the different results of the first sub-process ("Order placed" or "Rejection sent") visible on the upper level, an exclusive gateway is used. It selects the sequence flow according to the sub-process's result.

Like normal sub-processes, choreography sub-processes can also be aborted by catching intermediate events which are attached to their boundaries (cf. chapter 8.1). It is also possible to model event sub-processes in choreographies (cf. chapter 8.5).

11.4 Gateways in Choreographies

Besides the event-based exclusive gateway, it is also possible to use the normal, data-based gateways in a choreography. In figure 165, an exclusive gateway has been used. Inclusive, parallel, and complex gateways can also occur in a choreography.

The conditions at a gateway can only refer to contents of messages that have been exchanged earlier in the process. It is not possible to include other data for the decision. After all, a choreography only reflects the logic of the involved partners' processes. Actually, the decisions are taken in these partners' processes. Based on the result of a decision, different messages are sent. In the example, the decision is indeed only based on the exchanged messages. "Order placed" will be true if a message with an order has been exchanged. The condition "Rejection sent" will be fulfilled if a message with a rejection has been sent instead.

The data required for a decision must also be known to those partners who initiate the choreography activities directly after the gateway. Otherwise, they would not know whether they have to send a message.

As in normal processes, a default exit of an inclusive or an exclusive gateway can be defined by marking the outgoing sequence flow with a diagonal slash. For a choreography activity, it is also possible to have outgoing conditional sequence flows.

11.5 Events in Choreographies

In principle, it is possible to use not only untyped start and end events in choreographies, but also events with specific types of triggers, and intermediate events.

Triggers for start events can be signals, timer and multiple. Multiple start events are only allowed to combine signals and timers. Each participant can receive a broadcasted signal, and each can determine when a timer event occurs. Thus, all participants know about the occurrence of such an event, so that they can commence their common activities. Conditional events are also permitted, but only in event sub-processes. Signals, timer events, and multiple events may also be used for triggering an event sub-process.

There are only two possible end event types: The untyped event and the terminate event. When using a terminate event, it is important that all participants are informed of the termination during the preceding choreography-activity. Otherwise, the participants in parallel paths would not know about the termination and that they must not continue.

Normal sequence flows in choreographies can contain intermediate events of the following types: None, timer, conditional, link, signal, and multiple. When using a conditional intermediate event, it must be ensured that each participant has all information which is necessary to determine whether this event has occurred. Message events are not allowed since message flows are already covered by choreography activities.

In order to abort a choreography activity, a catching intermediate event can be attached to its boundary. For this purpose, timer and conditional events, as well as signals and multiple events can be used. Thereby it must be ensured that all concerned participants learn about the occurrence of the respective event. It is also possible to attach message, cancel, or compensation events; however they must be attached to the band of that participant that receives the event. For an attached message intermediate event, the message must be sent by another participant who is also involved in the same choreography activity.

11.6 Calling Choreographies and Global Choreography Tasks

In chapter 7.5 the concept of the call activity was explained, which can be used for calling a global task or a process defined elsewhere.

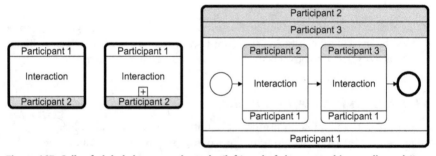

Figure 167: Calls of global choreography tasks (left) and of choreographies – collapsed (center) and expanded (right)

The same concept is also available for choreographies. The border of a choreography activity which is used for a call is drawn with a thick line (figure 167). It can either call a global choreography task (left) or another choreography. A global choreography task is defined once and can be re-used in several choreographies. The call of another, independent choreography can either be shown in a collapsed (center) or expanded call activity (right).

11.7 Use of Choreographies and Collaborations

As explained at the beginning of the chapter, the contents of a choreography can also be expressed by a collaboration. However, there are some reasons for using choreographies:

- In a choreography, the representation of message exchanges is independent from the partners' processes. This is a better basis for agreements and contracts between partners. Based on a choreography, the required process interfaces of the partners can be developed. Thus, it provides a starting point for designing or adapting each partner's individual process so that the agreed cooperation is supported correctly.
- The sequence of message exchanges, including splits etc., becomes more clearly visible. In a collaboration, this information is not explicit, but it needs to be derived from one of the involved partner's processes.
- Especially for large scenarios, the representation as a choreography is more compact and clear than a collaboration with at least one public process.
- Choreographies can be decomposed into choreography sub-processes. This also supports a compact and understandable presentation.
- If a complex scenario is modeled only with collaborations, it will be difficult to verify whether the processes' behaviors match. Deadlocks may occur, e.g. if two processes both wait for a message from each other. Choreography diagrams can be more easily analyzed with respect to the feasibility of the message exchanges.

Especially for complex business-to-business scenarios, choreography diagrams can be interesting, e.g. in the context of electronic marketplaces or for developing industry standards and guidelines for handling certain business transactions between partners.

However, if a company develops its internal processes and wants to show the message exchange with partners, usually a collaboration diagram will be the first choice.

12 Conversations

12.1 Conversation Diagrams

A conversation diagram provides an overview of which partners of a certain domain co-operate on which tasks. In figure 168, three conversations can be seen. When processing an order for an advertisement, one customer works together with one advertising agency and several designers. On the other hand, a customer and an advertising agency can jointly run an advertising campaign. For this, they co-operate with several media. A designer can also be part of another inter-company activity: Together with a publisher, he handles orders for illustrations.

In the end, such a conversation is realized by a series of message flows. The details can be modeled e.g. in a choreography diagram or a collaboration diagram. As an example, the message flow of the conversation "Process Order for Advertisement" is described by the collaboration diagram in figure 159, as well as by the choreography diagram in figure 160. However, it is not required for a collaboration or choreography diagram to specify exactly one conversation. It is also possible to combine the message flows from two or more conversations in one diagram.

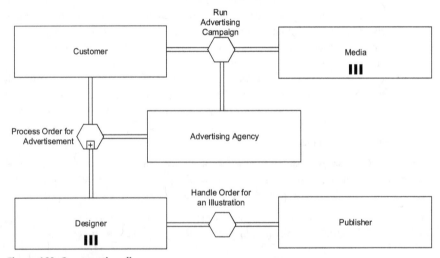

Figure 168: Conversation diagram

138

12.2 Message Correlations

The contents of the message flows within one conversation are always related to each other. For example, all messages that are exchanged within one instance of the conversation "Process Order for Advertisement" relate to the same advertisement order. It is, therefore, possible to use the order ID for the correlation, i.e. the assignment of messages to a process instance. If a customer receives an advertisement for approval, he can determine the corresponding order – and thus the process instance – based on the order ID. All messages of a conversation have a common correlation.

The connection between a conversation and a participant is called conversation link. A conversation is always connected to two or more participants.

It is possible that there are several partners of the same type involved in a conversation. "Process Order for Advertisement" has exactly one customer and one advertising agency as participants, but multiple designers. Therefore, the designer's pool contains a multiple marker. However, it is not clear which conversations have several partners of the same type. For example, the participant "Designer" is also connected with the conversation "Handle Order for an Illustration". Maybe in this conversation, there is only one designer involved. If such information is important, more detailed collaboration or choreography diagrams are required.

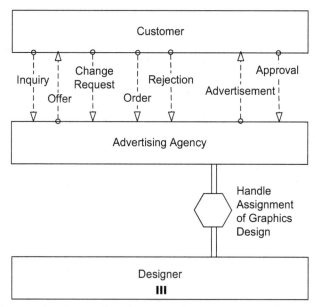

Figure 169: Conversation diagram for sub-conversation "Process Order for Advertisement"

12.3 Hierarchies of Conversations

Conversations can be further detailed using sub-conversations. Similar to sub-processes they are marked with a '+'-sign. The details of a sub-conversation can be described in another conversation diagram. The diagram of a sub-conversation can only contain those participants who are linked to the sub-conversation within the parent diagram.

Figure 169 shows the detailed conversation diagram for the sub-conversation "Process Order for Advertisement" As can be seen from this diagram, it is also possible to draw message flows directly into the conversation diagram. Other than collaboration diagrams, conversation diagrams are not allowed to show processes in the pools or choreographies between the pools.

The diagram contains those message flows that are related to the same order. To be more precise, they relate to the same inquiry. In the beginning, an order has not been placed yet, and not every inquiry turns into an order. Therefore, the common reference point is the inquiry.

Besides the explicitly displayed message flows between customer and advertising agency, the diagram also contains the conversation "Handle Assignment of Graphics Design". All message flows of this conversation are also related to the same inquiry, but this information is not sufficient for the advertising agency in order to assign all incoming messages correctly. This is because availability requests are sent to several designers. The advertising agency has to assign each incoming availability notice to the correct availability request. Thus, additional information is required for correlating these messages, e.g. the IDs of the availability requests. Therefore, it is possible to define a separate Conversation for the message flows between the advertising agency and the designers.

The message exchanges of this conversation can also be modeled in a collaboration diagram (figure 170) or a choreography diagram (figure 171). Of course, it is also possi-

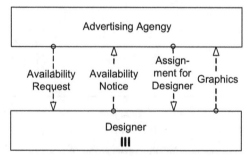

Figure 170: Collaboration diagram for conversation "Handle Assignment of Graphics Design"

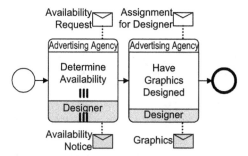

Figure 171: Choreography diagram for conversation "Handle Assignment of Graphics Design"

ble to show the message flows of the entire sub-conversation within a single diagram (figures 159 and 160 in the previous chapter).

Like sub-processes, sub-conversations can also be expanded, i.e. the hexagon is enlarged, and the detailed conversation is shown in its interior. However, it is graphically not easy to include, for example, the contents of figure 169 into an expanded sub-conversation in figure 168. Unfortunately, the BPMN specification draft does not contain any examples for expanded sub-conversations either.

12.4 Calling Global Conversations and Collaborations

Similar to processes and choreographies it is possible within conversation diagrams to call global conversations. A global conversation is defined independently from the conversation diagram from which it is called. A global conversation is specified by its own, independent conversation diagram. The border of a calling conversation is drawn with a thick line (figure 172).

Since a called conversation is defined elsewhere, it may be necessary to map its participants and correlation information to the participants and correlation information of the conversation diagram from which it is called. This, however, is mainly a topic for automating inter-company processes. In business-oriented diagrams, such mappings can be deduced from the context, or they are explained by annotations.

Figure 172: Calls of a collaboration (left) and a global conversation (right)

12.5 Use of Conversation Diagrams

For most BPMN modelers, the exact definition of correlations and thus the modeling of conversations will not be a primary concern. In the context of platforms for SOA (Service-Oriented Architecture) and process engines for supporting complex inter-company processes between several partners, on the other hand, this topic can be quite important. For such problems, conversations can provide a useful view of the entire scenario.

In many other cases, detailed correlation mechanisms are not of interest, but a conversation diagram can still be useful for the first overview of a network of partners. It can be seen which partners communicate with each other about which topics and business transactions. The details can then be modeled in choreography diagrams and collaboration diagrams.

13 Artifacts and Extensions of BPMN

13.1 Artifacts

BPMN models are focused on sequence and message flows, and on exchanged data. If other aspects relevant to a business process need to be mapped, it is possible to use artifacts.

So far, the BPMN specification has defined three standard types of artifacts: Annotations, groups, and associations. In addition to these, modelers and tool vendors are free to define their own artifacts, thus complementing BPMN with required constructs.

Annotations and groups have already been used in several examples, e.g. in figure 10 and figure 146.

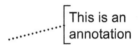

Figure 173: Annotation

An annotation is used for adding explanations, remarks, etc. to a certain model element (figure 173). Thus, annotations increase the understanding of a model. They do not have any effect on the control flow logic of the model.

On the other hand, annotations can also be used for documenting exit conditions of a loop, for example (cf. figure 110). The exit conditions themselves naturally do have an effect on the control flow logic of the process. In BPMN, however, the exit conditions, etc. are rather defined by attribute values of the respective modeling elements. The presentation in the model by annotations is only for documentation purposes. Usually, they are not evaluated, e.g. by process engines.

An annotation is represented by an opening square bracket. It can be connected with any element in a BPMN model via a dotted association, e.g. for adding a comment or explanation to this element.

Associations must be distinguished from sequence and message flows. The representation by a dotted line is the same as that of a data association. The BPMN specification indeed differentiates between associations and data associations, but this difference is mainly relevant in the context of process execution. If the direction is relevant, an association can also be drawn with an arrow. Such a directed association is used for assigning a compensation activity to another activity (cf. figure 147).

Figure 174: Group

A group is drawn as a rounded rectangle. Its border consists of a line of dots and dashes (figure 174). The dots and dashes must be clearly visible. Otherwise, it could be confused with a sub-process.

Like all artifacts, a group is purely a graphical object without any relevance for the logic of a BPMN diagram. Therefore, it is possible to use it without any restrictions, for highlighting interesting parts of a model, or for grouping elements which are related to each other. It is also allowed to draw groups across the borders of pools and lanes. As a purely graphical element, a group cannot be the source or the target of a sequence or message flow. Flows can rather cross group borders as desired.

13.2 How to Extend BPMN

As already mentioned, any BPMN construct can be graphically changed and adapted, as long as the original BPMN shape is still clearly recognizable and cannot be confused with other types of elements. For example, it is possible to use different colors and fonts. When using colors, it must be considered that some information is denoted by different shadings. In choreography activities, initiating partners are differentiated from the other partners by white and gray bands. When using other colors, the difference must be made clear by lighter and darker coloring.

Care must be taken, too, when changing line styles and widths, since these usually have a meaning. For example, an end event must have a thicker border than a start or intermediate event. Solid, dashed, and dotted lines must also be clearly visible, in order to distinguish between sequence flows, message flows, and associations. The solid borders of sub-processes and the dot and dash borders of groups must be preserved, as well.

The graphical symbols of modeling elements can be modified. However, the BPMN basic symbols must remain recognizable. An activity can be appended with an additional icon, but it must still be represented by a rounded rectangle. Likewise, the envelope symbol of a message event must not be replaced by an entirely different symbol. It must also remain visible whether the symbol in an event is filled or blank because this depicts the difference between throwing and catching events.

Furthermore, additional attributes can be defined for BPMN elements. This is especially interesting because the pre-defined attributes are mainly used for execution by a process engine. More business-related attributes, such as cost rates, can be added via BPMN's extension mechanism.

Eventually, it is also possible to define additional artifacts and connect them to the existing BPMN elements via associations. Maybe it is required to show which services are provided by an activity, or which software application or machine is used for it. In many cases, the use of lanes for assigning organizational units or performing roles will not be sufficient. As an example, activities can be performed jointly by several people, or it needs to be differentiated between a role which is responsible for an activity and one which performs this activity.

The BPMN standard does not yet provide specific constructs for integrating such elements from other views of an enterprise model. By using self-defined artifacts, it is easy to create this connection. BPMN explicitly allows for connecting artifacts with objects from other types of models, such as organizational charts or UML diagrams. When using a modeling tool, it needs to be checked whether it already contains such extensions. Alternatively, it may allow for the definition of individual artifacts.

The described possibilities for extending BPMN are such that everybody who knows the BPMN standard can understand an extended BPMN model without any problems. Only the additional information contained in the individual extensions will not be clear to him without additional explanation.

However, if many individual extensions are used, it may be the case that a large portion of relevant information is contained in these extensions. In this case, many advantages of using a standard get lost, such as the common understanding and the exchangeability with other tools.

14 BPMN Modeling Patterns

Process modelers repeatedly encounter similar situations and problems. Modeling patterns are proposals how to model such recurring cases. Instead of developing a specific solution every time, it is often possible to re-use existing and proven solutions. A common patterns catalog in an enterprise helps the modelers to represent the same things always in the same way. This makes the models better understandable.

It is therefore recommended to develop such collections of patterns and to continuously add new patterns that are detected in daily modeling. Depending on the application domain and the modeling purpose, there may be very different kinds of patterns.

In the following paragraphs, some general modeling patterns are presented. These patterns address problems that are relevant to many companies. Some of these patterns have been developed together with BPMN trainers from AXON IVY AG, Switzerland.

14.1 Four Eyes Principle

The four eyes principle is used for important documents, letters, proposals, etc. They must not be created and released by the same person. Instead, the item needs to be reviewed by someone else. This policy helps to ensure that company guidelines are followed, that errors are detected at an early stage, and that fraud is prevented.

The application of this principle in a process is easy to model (figure 175). After a document has been written by the author, it is reviewed by another person. If this person approves the content, the document is released. Otherwise, the author reworks the document, before it is reviewed again.

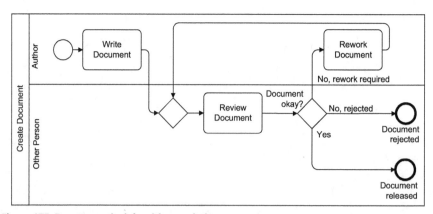

Figure 175: Four eyes principle with cancelation

Instead of a document, the created object can also be a proposal, a contract, a calculation, or something similar.

In this pattern, it is important that the two roles represented by the lanes actually need to be performed by different persons. In many other processes it is perfectly acceptable that one single person performs two or more roles, but here this must be prevented. Therefore, the lower lane explicitly has been labeled with "Other Person". When this pattern is used in a specific process in which the lanes need to have other labels (such as "Developer" and "Quality Inspector"), an annotation can be used for documenting that these roles must be performed by different persons.

At a closer look, the model in figure 175 has a shortcoming. If the author and the reviewer do not eventually agree that the document can be released, the two tasks "Review Document" and "Rework Document" are repeatedly carried out in an endless loop. In practice, the participants will quit this loop after a while – although this is not explicitly defined in the model.

To model this more precisely, a third exit can be added to the splitting gateway. The sequence flow from this exit leads to a second end event that marks the unsuccessful outcome. This is shown in figure 176. Here, the other person can decide that the document is entirely rejected. It would also be possible to let the author decide whether he wants to withdraw the document. This could be modeled with another gateway after "Rework Document" with one exit leading to an end event.

This pattern can easily be extended. For example, the four eyes principle could be extended to a six eyes principle by adding another review by a third person. This second review can be carried out in parallel to the first review, as it is modeled in the pattern "Parallel Checks" (chapter 14.4). In another variation, a possible disagreement between the author and the reviewer could be solved by routing these cases to a second check that is carried out by a third person.

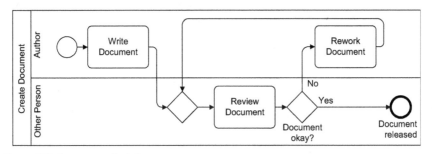

Figure 176: Four eyes principle

147

14.2 Decisions in Sub-Processes

Sub-processes often have several alternative end events which lead to different paths in the parent process. The pattern "Decision in Sub-Process" makes clear how the selected path is related to the result of the decision that has been made in the sub-process. This pattern has already been used in the discussion of sub-processes in chapter 7.1 (figure 107).

The sub-process can contain any arbitrary flow. The sub-process "Evaluate Proposal" in figure 177 is just an example. For the pattern it is important that each possible end result of the sub-process is represented by a separate end event. If the same results can be created in different parts of the sub-processes, they are combined into one end event. For example, in figure 177 the two "No" branches end in the common end event "Proposal rejected". All end events are positioned near the right border of the sub-process.

In the parent process, the sub-process is followed by a splitting exclusive gateway. This gateway has one exit for each of the sub-process's end events. The labels at the gateway exits indicate which path relates to which end event. In figure 177, the gateway is labeled with a question. Each answer to this question makes clear which result is being referred to. As an alternative, the question at the gateway can be omitted, and the outgoing branches can be labeled with the names of the end events (figure 178).

In both cases, it is also useful to sort the branches from top to bottom in the same order as the end events in the sub-process. Thus, the top branch refers to the top end event, etc.

Instead of a gateway, it is also possible to use conditional sequence flows. In this case, the sequence flows that are related to the sub process's end events start directly at the sub-process border (figure 179). If the expanded view of the sub-process is shown in

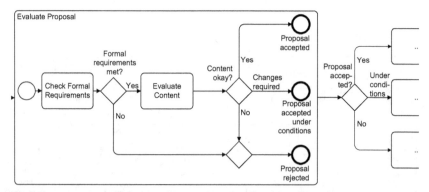

Figure 177: For each of the sub process's end events, there is one corresponding exit at the exclusive gateway

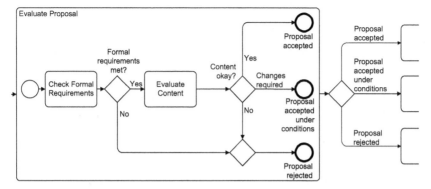

Figure 178: The gateway's exits are labelled with the names of the sub-process's end events

the diagram, the start of each sequence flow can be drawn directly next to an end event, so that it looks like the continuation of the respective sequence flow. Although the tokens in the sub-process and those in the parent process are different ones, there is a tight relation between them. The graphical layout reflects this relation.

14.3 Tasks with Multiple Actors

Typically, every task is performed by one actor. This is modeled by placing the task in the actor's lane. Sometimes, however, a task is jointly performed by several actors. This is difficult to model in BPMN since an activity can only be placed in one lane. It is not allowed to draw an activity symbol in a way that it spans several lanes.

There are several possible solutions to this problem (cf. [Chinosi 2012]). Two of these approaches are discussed in this section.

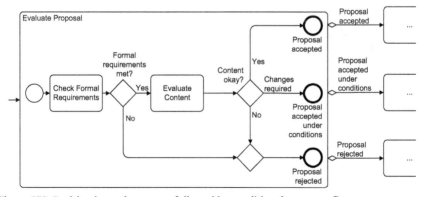

Figure 179: Decision in a sub-process, followed by conditional sequence flows

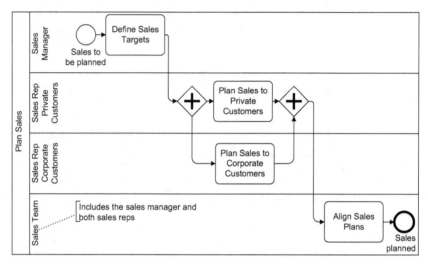

Figure 180: A separate lane is used for tasks that are carried out by several actors together

In the sales planning process in figure 180, each of the first three tasks is performed by one different role. The fourth task, "Align Sales Plans" is to be carried out by all three roles jointly.

Since activities are not allowed to span several lanes, a fourth lane has been introduced that represents the entire sales team. Tasks in this lane are carried out by all members of the team together. The diagram does not graphically show that the sales team consists of the other three lanes' actors. Therefore, an annotation has been added.

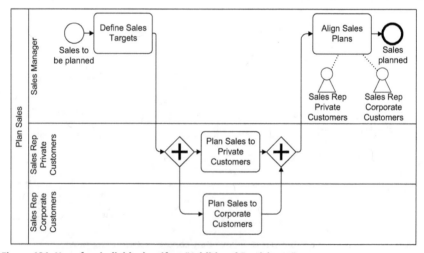

Figure 181: Use of an individual artifact "Additional Participant"

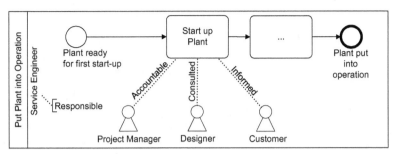

Figure 182: Different types of participation in a task

Another way of modeling tasks with multiple actors is proposed in [Freund and Schrepfer 2012]. It makes use of individual artifacts. In figure 181, the joint task has been placed in the sales manager's lane. The two different sales representatives have been modeled using artifact of the type "Additional Participant". They are connected with the task via associations. The artifact "Additional Participant" is not part of the BPMN standard, but an individual extension. As explained in chapter 13.1, BPMN explicitly allows for such additional artifacts.

The additional participants in figure 181 are labeled with the same names as the two lower lanes so that it becomes clear that they represent the same roles as these lanes. The three participants and their assignments to the task are now depicted in rather different ways. The sales manager's assignment is represented by placing the task in his lane while the other participants are represented by small person icons. This raises the question for which of a task's participants a lane should be used, and for which the newly introduced artifact. In most cases, the lane is used for that participant that plays a leading role in carrying out the task.

Very often there are different ways of participating in an activity. They can be classified according to RACI. The letters of this acronym stand for the types of involvement:

R	Responsible	Doing the actual work
A	Accountable	Delegating the task and approving its results
C	Consulted	Providing expertise and advice
I	Informed	Being kept up-to-date on the activity and its results

When using the "Additional Participant" artifact, it can be defined that the responsible role is represented by the lane, while the other roles are modeled as additional participants. Their associations to the task can be labeled with the types of involvement, as it is shown in figure 182.

For using this way of representing multiple actors, it is important to select a modeling tool that provides the possibility to define individual artifacts. There are also modeling tools on the market which already have pre-defined artifacts for additional participants.

14.4 Parallel Checks

When different persons need to check applications, requests, etc. according to different criteria, these checks can be carried out in parallel. In chapter 6.3 an example with parallel checks has been used for discussing the terminate end event.

There is also a simpler way of modeling parallel checks, without terminate end events. Since each check can have a positive or negative result, there can be many different combinations of positive and negative results. If all these possible combinations are considered, the models quickly become large and confusing. However, in most cases it is not important exactly which of the checks have a positive or a negative outcome. Instead, only two cases need to be considered: Either all checks have a positive result, or at least one check has a negative result.

Therefore, in figure 183 the checking activities are not directly followed by exclusive splits. Instead, the parallel paths are joined before there is an exclusive split that distinguishes whether all checks have produced a positive result, or not.

In this model, all parallel checks are always carried out entirely, even if one of the checks has already had a negative result, and the other checks would not be required anymore.

This can be avoided using a terminate end event. Figure 184 shows the solution from chapter 6.3 (figure 84) again. This time, however, the parallel checks have been placed in a sub-process. This is necessary for enabling the process to continue after the terminate end event has been reached. If the terminate end event were part of the top process level, it would terminate the entire process. Since it is in the sub-process, only this sub-process is terminated, and the parent process continues according to the pattern "Decision in Subprocess", as described in chapter 14.2.

In this context, a remark may be useful, concerning the use of lanes in sub-processes. If the parallel checking tasks should be performed by different roles, it seems an obvious idea to place these sub-process tasks in different lanes. However, the entire sub-process itself is already situated exactly in one lane in the parent process. As a consequence, the contained tasks are also part of this lane and cannot be placed in other lanes. Especially

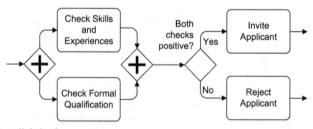

Figure 183: Parallel checks

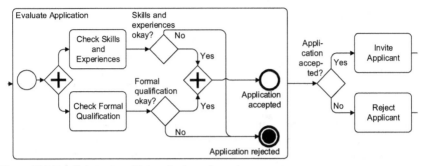

Figure 184: Parallel checks with terminate end event

when the sub-process is drawn in a separate diagram, this dependency is often overlooked, and wrongly further lanes are drawn.

One possibility is to use nested lanes, i.e. lanes that are partitioned into sub-lanes (see chapter 2.4). In the parent process, the sub-process is placed exactly in one lane. In the sub-process's diagram, this lane is then divided into further lanes. Another possibility is to use a call activity (cf chapter 7.5) and to call a separate process instead of a normal sub-process. Since a called process is a completely independent process, it can contain any arbitrary lanes.

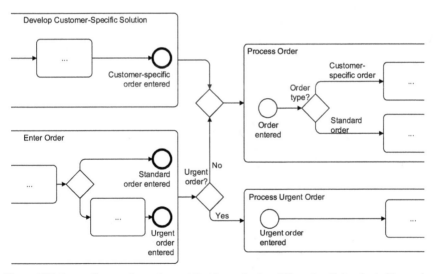

Figure 185: Depending on the end event that is reached, a different path is selected in a subsequent sub-process

14.5 Process Interfaces

Some process notations contain an element called "process interface". In processes with more than one end events, process interfaces can be used to indicate for each end event, which process will be triggered after reaching that end event. Process interfaces can also be used in front of start events in order to model which preceding process triggers this start event.

BPMN does not provide such an element. If the successional processes are entirely independent, they can be modeled in separate pools. The corresponding start and end events of the two processes can be modeled as message events and connected with a message flow.

If the two processes are sub-processes of the same parent process, there are no specific BPMN elements to mark this kind of connection. Considering the discussions in chapter 6.2, there are different ways how to model this.

If different sub-processes should be triggered, based on the preceding sub-processes' end events, then an exclusive splitting gateway is required in the parent process. This corresponds to the pattern "Decision in Sub-Process" (chapter 14.2).

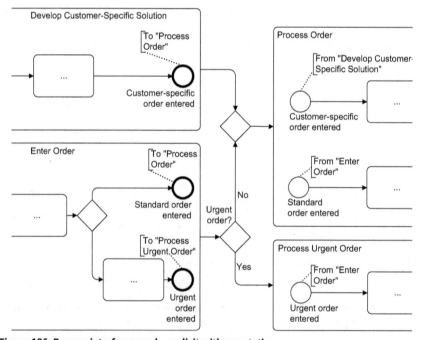

Figure 186: Process interfaces made explicit with annotations

The reaching of the end event "Standard order entered" in figure 185 causes the sub-process "Process Order" to be started. If "Urgent order entered" is reached instead, the sub-process "Process Urgent Order" is triggered.

If the first steps of the sub-process "Process Order" should vary, depending on the preceding sub-process, this can be achieved with a splitting gateway at the beginning. The labels on the gateway exit indicate the related end events of the preceding sub-processes.

There is another variation that shows the relationships between the corresponding events more clearly. Instead of a splitting gateway, in figure 186 the sub-processes "Process Order" contains two different "none" start events. For each start event, the name of the preceding process is shown in an annotation. There are also annotations attached to the end events, stating the names of corresponding succeeding processes.

14.6 Synchronizing Parallel Paths

The communication between different processes is modeled with message flows. For example, a catching intermediate message event is used to define that a process waits for a message and can only continue when another process has sent a message of a specific type. But how to model the same thing within one process? Message flows are only allowed between pools. They must not start and end in the same pool.

In most cases it is possible to use sequence flow and parallel gateways for modeling such waiting situations. In figure 187, the task "Develop Detailed Concept" in the upper path should not be started before "Provide Funding" has been completed in the lower path. This can easily be achieved with parallel gateways. In figure 188, the token from the lower path is duplicated at the parallel gateway. In the upper path, both the token from the upper path and one of the lower path's tokens need to arrive at the joining parallel gateway, before "Develop Detailed Concept" can be started.

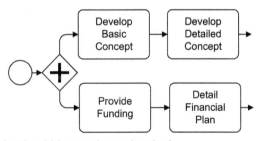

Figure 187: Parallel paths which are to be synchronized

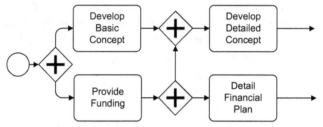

Figure 188: Synchronisation with parallel gateways

If there are many such synchronizations in a large diagram, it may become rather complex and difficult to understand.

It becomes really difficult if a communication is required between sub-processes because sequence flows must not cross the boundaries of sub-processes. Therefore, in figure 189, no sequence flow can be modeled between the lower and the upper path. Neither it is possible to use link events, as they have been discussed in chapter 6.4, since they are only layout elements that allow for interrupting the line that represents a sequence flow. It is not permitted to position a throwing link event in one subprocess, and the related catching link event in the other subprocess, since this would also establish a sequence flow crossing sub-process borders.

Sometimes it is proposed to use signal events for this problem. In the lower sub-process the task "Provide Funding" could be followed by a throwing intermediate signal event "Funding provided". In the upper sub-process, there could be a catching intermediate signal event after the task "Develop Basic Concept". The upper path then waits at this catching event for the arrival of the signal "Funding provided", before "Develop Detailed Concept" can be started.

Unfortunately, there is a problem with this solution. Other than messages which are always addressed to a specific receiver, signals are broadcasted everywhere. When the signal "Funding provided" is sent, it is not only received by the same process instance,

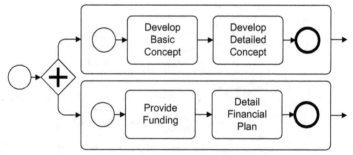

Figure 189: Synchronization using sequence flows is not possible for parallel flows from different sub-processes

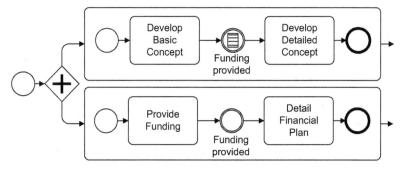

Figure 190: Synchronization with a conditional event

but by all instances of this process. This means that all other waiting process instances will also start developing a detailed concept, although their funding is not provided yet.

The proposed solution is shown in figure 190. The upper sub-process waits at the conditional event "Funding provided". This condition will be fulfilled when the task "Provide Funding" is completed in the lower sub-process. This has been visualized with a "none" intermediate event. It has no effect on the process flow, but it helps the reader to identify the connection between the two sub-processes.

If this pattern should be implemented as software, the task "Provide funding" can set the value of a boolean process variable to "true", while in the condition of the waiting event, the value of this variable is evaluated.

14.7 Requests with Different Types of Replies

The receiver of a message can send different types of answers in a collaboration. For example, a proposal can be accepted or rejected. Based on the received answer, different paths may be selected in the requestor's process.

There are two ways to model this situation. In figure 191, there are two message types that can be received after sending a request message, either an acceptance message or a rejection message. The two catching message events are preceded by an event-based gateway so that the upper path is selected when an acceptance message arrives while the lower path is selected when a rejection message arrives. This kind of modeling visualizes rather clearly which different types of answers can be sent.

In figure 192, the same case has been modeled in a different way. Here, the different possible answer types are not represented by different message types. Instead, there is only one message type "Reply". Whether the reply is an acceptance or a rejection is part of the message content. The catching message event is followed by a data-based

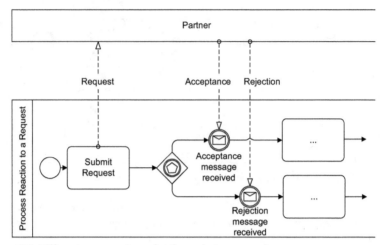

Figure 191: Different message types for the reply to a request

exclusive gateway which routes the arriving token according to the message content either to the upper or the lower path.

This kind of modeling represents the real process if the message exchange is not automated. Usually, the reply to a request arrives in an e-mail or a letter. Only when the e-mail or the letter is opened, and the content is read, it is known whether the request has been accepted or rejected. The model is also easier to understand for people who are not BPMN experts because they do not to know the semantics of the event-based gateway.

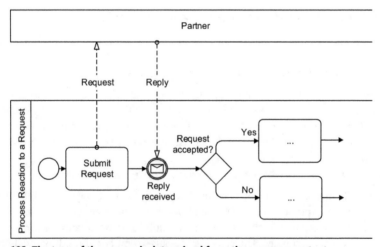

Figure 192: The type of the answer is determined from the message content

14.8 Processing Cancelations

How to cancel an order has already been described in connection with the introduction of attached intermediate events in chapter 8.1 and with the discussion of compensations in chapter 9.1. Therefore, the basic structure of the pattern in figure 193 is already known: The attached intermediate message event makes sure that after the arrival of a cancelation message, the entire sub-process will be terminated, and a token will flow to the exception sequence flow.

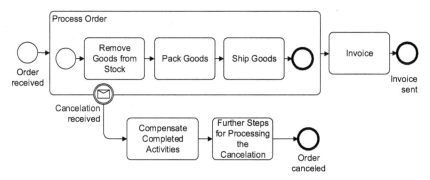

Figure 193: Cancelation

In chapter 9.1 it has been explained, how to use compensation activities for modeling how to reverse the effects of completed activities. There are not any compensation activities in figure 193. Instead, a general activity "Compensate Completed Activities" has been used. This is based on the assumption that the responsible performer can decide for himself what exactly needs to be done.

In many cases, it does not make sense to try to predict all possible situations in advance. This is especially true for exceptions and special cases. Therefore, these exceptions and special cases are forwarded to a qualified person who can analyze the situation and decide about the necessary steps.

However, if cancelations occur rather frequently in the above example, and the process control is fully automated, then it is useful to model the compensations exactly. It is then possible to process cancelations in a standardized way and just as efficiently as the normal flow.

14.9 Deadline Monitoring

The monitoring of deadlines is a typical use case for event-based gateways. The process in figure 194 sends a request to a partner. If the partner replies within the defined timespan, the reply is processed, and the process is finished. If the deadline is reached and no reply has been received, the event "Deadline reached" is triggered as the first of

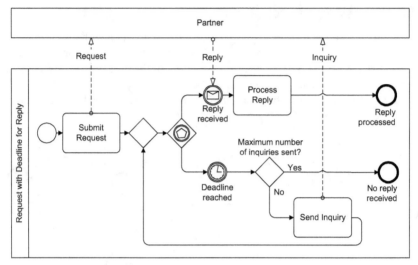

Figure 194: Deadline monitoring

the two intermediate events. If the number of inquiries is less than a defined maximum number, an inquiry is sent, and the process waits again for a reply.

If the maximum number of inquiries has been reached, the process ends unsuccessfully. In this case, the company may look for another partner. Such activities are not part of this pattern anymore. Without defining a maximum number of inquiries, it would be possible that new inquiries would be sent endlessly if the partner does not answer.

This pattern can be combined with the pattern "Request with Different Types of Replies" which has been described in chapter 14.7. If the variant with different message types is used, additional catching message events need to be added after the event-based gateway. For the other variant, with just one message type, a data-based exclusive gateway can be inserted after the message event "Reply received". The exit of this splitting gateway is chosen according to the content of the reply message.

14.10 Dunning Procedure

The principle of the pattern "Deadline Monitoring" can also be used for modeling a multi-level dunning procedure. Instead of separately modeling the flows for the first reminder, the second reminder, etc., a loop is used in figure 195. Every time the loop is repeated, the current dunning level and the deadline for this level are determined, before the next reminder is sent.

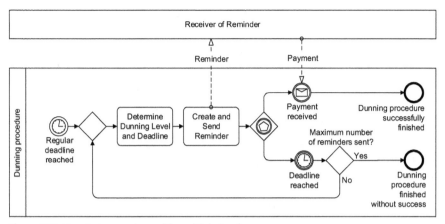

Figure 195: Dunning procedure with multiple levels

The process then waits at the event-based gateway for the payment. If the deadline is reached before a payment has been received, the next step depends on whether the maximum number of reminders has already been sent. If this is not the case, the next dunning level is reached, and another reminder is sent. If the maximum number of reminders is reached, the dunning procedure is finished without success. This usually triggers further actions, such as taking legal actions.

The model does neither show the dunning levels nor the actual timespan for the deadline. This information is transmitted to the receiver of the reminder in the content of the reminder message. The advantage of this pattern is that it represents a dunning procedure with any number of levels in a rather concise way.

14.11 Call for Proposals

A call for proposals is sent to multiple suppliers. Until a defined deadline, each supplier can submit a proposal. Then the best proposal is selected.

The model in figure 196 again is similar to the deadline monitoring pattern. In contrast to that pattern, here the call for proposals is not sent to one, but to several suppliers.

This is done in a multi-instance activity. The supplier pool is marked as multi-instance participant since it represents the group of all involved suppliers.

After sending the call for proposals, the process waits at the event-based gateway for the arrival of proposals. Each time a proposal arrives, it is registered, and the waiting for proposals continues. When the time event "Deadline for proposals reached" occurs, the best proposal is selected, and the process is finished.

Proposals that arrive after the submitting deadline are not considered anymore.

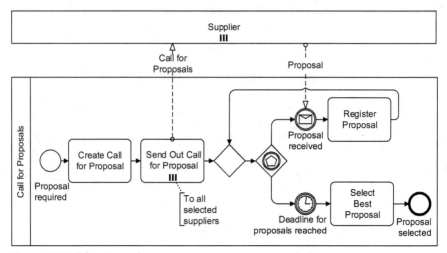

Figure 196: Call for proposals

The pattern can be varied. For example, it could be combined with the pattern "Deadline Monitoring", so that after the deadline has been reached, an inquiry is sent to those suppliers who have not sent a proposal yet.

A Bibliography

Allweyer T (2012) Human-Readable BPMN Diagrams. In: Fischer L (Ed.) BPMN 2.0 Handbook. 2nd Ed., Future Strategies, Lighthouse Point, p. 217-232

Chinosi M (2012) Collaborative Activities Inside Pools. In: Fischer L (Ed.) BPMN 2.0 Handbook. 2nd Ed., Future Strategies, Lighthouse Point, p. 151-164

Debevoise T, Taylor J (2014) The MicroGuide to Process and Decision Modeling in BPMN/DMN: Building More Effective Processes by Integrating Process Modeling with Decision Modeling. BookSurge, Charleston

Fischli S, Fischer M, Hadrian D, Lienhard H, Mayer E, Meister B, Schaffroth M (2016) Geschäftsprozesse grafisch darstellen – Der Einsatz von BPMN aus Geschäftssicht. eCH-0074. Version 2.1. Verein eCH, Zürich http://www.ech.ch/vechweb/page?p=dossier&documentNumber=eCH-0074&documentVersion=2.1

Freund J, Rücker B (2014) Real-Life BPMN – Using BPMN 2.0 to Analyze, Improve, and Automate Processes in Your Company. 2nd Ed., CreateSpace, Charleston

Freund J, Schrepfer M (2012) Best Practice Guidelines for BPMN 2.0. In: Fischer L (Ed.) BPMN 2.0 Handbook. 2nd Ed., Future Strategies, Lighthouse Point, p. 203-215

Grosskopf A, Decker G, Weske M (2009) The Process. Business Modeling Using BPMN. Meghan-Kiffer, Tampa

Herrera E (2015) The BPMN Graphic Handbook. CreateSpace, Charleston

ISO (2013) ISO/IEC 19510:2013: Information technology – Object Management Group Business Process Model and Notation http://standards.iso.org/ittf/PubliclyAvailableStandards/c062652_ISO_IEC_19510_2013.zip

Kossak F, Illibauer C, Geist V, Kubovy J, Natschläger C, Ziebermayr T, Kopetzky T, Freudenthaler B, Schewe K (2014) A Rigorous Semantics for BPMN 2.0 Process Diagrams. Springer, Cham Heidelberg New York Dordrecht London

Lindner S (2014) NRS Business Process Standards and Guidelines using BPMN. British Columbia Corporate Services for the Natural Resource Sector Information Management Branch http://www2.gov.bc.ca/assets/gov/british-columbians-and-our-governments/services-policies-for-government/information-technology/standards/natural-resource-sector/sdlc/standards/nrs_business_process_standards_and_guidelines.pdf

Lübbe A, Schnägelberger S (2015) BPM Toolmarktmonitor 2015. Umfrage unter Anwendern von BPM Software für Design & Analyse von Geschäftsprozessen. BPM&O, Köln

OASIS (2007) Web Services Business Process Execution Language Version 2.0. OASIS Standard
http://docs.oasis-open.org/wsbpel/2.0/OS/wsbpel-v2.0-OS.pdf

OMG (2013) Business Process Model and Notation (BPMN). Version 2.0.2. OMG Document Number: formal/2013-12-09
http://www.omg.org/spec/BPMN/2.0.2/

Queensland Government Chief Information Office (2016): BPMN 2.0 Guideline. Recommended Business Process Model and Notation 2.0 Elements. V3.0.0
https://www.qgcio.qld.gov.au/products/qgea-documents/547-business/3518-business-process-model-and-notation-bpmn

Silver B (2012) BPMN Method and Style. With BPMN Implementer's Guide. 2nd Ed., Cody-Cassidy Press, Aptos

Stiehl V (2014) Process-Driven Applications with BPMN. Springer, Cham Heidelberg New York Dordrecht London

Workflow Management Coalition (2012) Process Definition Interface – XML Process Definition Language. Document Number WFMC-TC-1025. Version 2.2
http://www.xpdl.org/standards/xpdl-2.2/XPDL%202.2%20(2012-08-30).pdf

B BPMN in the Internet

BPMN.org

> OMG's BPMN website. Besides the official BPMN specification, there are some introductory articles, examples, and web links.
>
> http://www.bpmn.org

BPMN Poster

> A poster with a BPMN 2.0 overview. Available in many different languages. Created by BPM Offensive Berlin.
>
> http://www.bpmb.de/index.php/BPMNPoster

BPMN Tool Matrix

> Comprehensive list of BPMN tools with information such as supported operating systems, release dates and license types.
>
> https://bpmnmatrix.github.io

Method & Style

> Bruce Silver's weblog on about BPMN and related standards, such as DMN (Decision Model and Notation) and CMMN (Case Management Model and Notation).
>
> http://methodandstyle.com/blog

Workflow Patterns

> Homepage of the Workflow Patterns Initiative, coordinated by Professor Wil van der Aalst (Eindhoven University of Technology) and Professor Arthur te Hofstede (Queensland University of Technology). Here, descriptions of differrent workflow patterns can be found, as well as articles on how to model the patterns in BPMN.
>
> http://www.workflowpatterns.com

Groups in Social Networks

> There are several BPMN-related groups in LinkedIn, XING, and Facebook.

Index

The Author

Thomas Allweyer studied Engineering at Stuttgart University and Brunel University (West London). He earned his doctoral degree at the Institue for Information Systems at the University of Saarland (Saarbrücken, Germany).

At IDS Scheer AG (now a division of Software AG) he was a product manager for the ARIS modeling tools and a consultant. After that, he became process manager at emaro AG, a joint venture of Deutsche Bank and SAP. Currently, he is a professor for enterprise modeling at Hochschule Kaiserslautern (University of Applied Sciences).

Thomas Allweyer is the author of several papers and books on business process management and process automation. Besides his university activities he is also a consultant, and he frequently holds seminars for well-known companies, especially on business process management – and BPMN, of course.

In his weblog he regularly blogs about current developments in business process management (*www.kurze-prozesse.de*, in German).